MW01076643

Quest and Crew

David Beaupré

Published by buddha bees

cover design and graphics by David Beaupré

Quest and Crew
© 2014 David Beaupré

Published by buddha bees

"How many people have dreamed about sailing away and leaving it all behind? Here's how it happened... On a clear starry night, we left South Florida on a dream enveloped by a hope."

The Quest Series
by David Beaupré

Quest and Crew
Quest on the Thorny Path
Quest for the Virgins
Quest in the Caribbean

Quest and Crew is a work of non-fiction. All places, characters, and events are real. In some cases the names of characters have been altered.

All rights reserved. This book was published by buddha bees. No part of this book may be used or reproduced in any manner without written permission except in the case of brief quotations embodied in critical articles and reviews.

ISBN-13: 978-0692223352   **buddha bees**

ISBN-10: 0692223355

Introduction to Quest and Crew

How many people have dreamed about sailing away and leaving it all behind? Here's how it happened. 'Quest and Crew' is the first book of a four book series. The story begins hours before a devastating Category 5 hurricane obliterates the south shore of Grenada. It's a story about the many twists and turns that life can take. The sailboat Quest gained a new lease on life with a complete retrofit in the backwoods of North Carolina. The job of the crew becoming real sailors began in North Palm Beach. On a clear starry night, we left South Florida on a hope enveloped by a dream. Finding ourselves at the beginning of a new adventure, we set sail and anchored one island at a time through the Bahamas. The Caribbean is a few books away. Here is a glimpse into the powerful attraction of sailboats and sapphire water. 'Quest and Crew' is all about the joy of success as well as what it takes to overcome the occasional disaster. From beginning to end, the book is about transforming a rookie crew and beautiful old boat into a sailing adventure. Come for the hurricane, stay for the story.

Introduction to The Quest Series

My wife and I are very fortunate to have followed a path in life that brings us closer to our dreams and to each other. It's nice work when you can get it. From the day we met, our lives have been filled with extraordinary experiences. Somewhere in a lifetime of memorable adventures we purchased a classic sailboat. Little did we guess the implications of preparing Quest and her crew for a life on the ocean. Learning our lessons along the way, Wendy and I were slowly transformed into sailors. From launching Quest in north Florida to a Category 5 hurricane in Grenada, we discover that the art of living on a sailboat is much more than rum-infused beach parties. It was hard work to have fun. But when all the chores are done and the storms have passed, Wendy and I consider ourselves fortunate to have fulfilled our dreams. Everyone can learn to be the master of their destiny. If time does not permit you to sail the ocean blue, I offer you this four book series on how two friends found happiness in their personal quest for paradise. The Quest Series is a true modern sailing story. Come along, let's take this extraordinary journey together.

Introduction to Quest on the Thorny Path

Not all trips to paradise are smooth sailing. 'Quest on the Thorny Path' is the second book of the Quest series. Leave the laid back cruiser hangout of Georgetown, Bahamas behind and hit the big ocean waves for the first time. From Georgetown we take the path less traveled through the deserted out islands of the Bahamas. After a short stay in the Turks and Caicos we follow a route along the north coast of Hispaniola that Christopher Columbus appropriately named the 'Thorny Path'. The book is a true adventure about overcoming fear and dangerous challenges in one of sailing's harshest proving grounds. Bashing through heavy seas and strong headwinds on a lee shore isn't for everyone. But at least you can read about it.

Introduction to Quest for the Virgins

Find our crew poised and ready to venture into the dreaded Mona Passage between Hispaniola and Puerto Rico. We're on our way for a long, leisurely sail on the beautiful south coast of Puerto Rico. It is my pleasure to have you come along for the third book in the Quest series. Included in the itinerary is Vieques, St. Croix, St. John and a little Virgin Gorda. With a unique perspective for the almost unnoticed, 'Quest for the Virgins' will deliver a less common experience of a most popular place. Be whisked away to warm tropical destinations for a humorous glimpse into the life aboard a sailboat in the Caribbean.

Introduction to Quest in the Caribbean

The final book in the Quest series is 'Quest in the Caribbean'. Wendy and I have become full time sailors. The sea has been kind to us. It has been our home, a very strict master and unforgiving teacher. We slowly learned our lessons of seamanship one day at a time. But more importantly we learned a great deal about each other and what it takes to be good companions on a tiny boat. 'Quest for the Caribbean' begins on a beautiful day in the British Virgin Islands. When we pass through the dangerous, narrow, reef-strewn passage in Virgin Gorda and enter the Caribbean we are just one boat length closer to fulfilling our dream. There are many more islands to explore and miles to sail before the journey is complete. Some of the wonders that await our eager eyes are Saba, the fabled 'island in the clouds' and the neighboring island of Statia. The serenely beautiful island of Nevis, Montserrat's volcanoes, the gentle people of Dominica, Saint Lucia and the Grenadines all enrich our lives. 'Quest for the Caribbean' ends on the south shore of Grenada as we are about to fulfill a destiny that was many hard years in the making.

David Beaupré
Fall River, Tennessee

Contents

One

Quest vs. Ivan: A Heavyweight Match

In the fall of 2004 Wendy and I were happy living our island dream on the south coast of Grenada. We had comfortable dockage for our sailboat Quest at a newly constructed marina. We were happy and safe from the dangers of hurricanes. Life was good in paradise.

On the morning of September 11th we drove to a chandlery in Saint George to order a few boat parts. As was his custom in hurricane season, Tony the owner was sitting in front of his PC. Tony was the local VHF radio weather man.

"Checking the weather?" I joked.

"Yeah" he said. "Take a look at this."

His computer screen showed a very distinct circulation just off Cape Verde. The desert heat blowing west from Africa spawns many Caribbean hurricanes.

"This looks very serious. Tropical storms don't usually form so close to Africa. If this gains momentum it's going to be huge" he said.

For the hundreds of liveaboard cruisers in Grenada, hurricanes were weather events that happened some where else. Hurricanes never hit Grenada. Hurricanes never go below 12 degrees latitude. Insurance companies universally agreed that the south coast of Grenada was below the hurricane belt. Boat owners were encouraged to keep their boats on the south coast of Grenada during hurricane season. History, and actuarial tables, were about to be rewritten.

On the following morning the tropical depression that had rapidly formed off the African coast had suddenly developed into a tropical storm. It was moving at the unusually fast ground speed of 25 knots. The tropical storm was such a well organized system that the long range models predicted a very strong hurricane hitting Martinique. As the day progressed the intensity of the storm increased to a hurricane Category 1. By two o'clock, Ivan was a Category 2. It was incomprehensible how fast the storm was gaining strength. Ivan was aimed lower at Saint Lucia. Our thoughts strayed to the great times we had in Rodney Bay on Saint Lucia. We counted our blessings that we were safe. By seven o'clock that evening Ivan had developed some real teeth. It was a solid Category 3 and building rapidly. The ground speed had slowed to 20 knots and it started to curve south. It was almost unheard of for a hurricane to veer south. Hurricanes usually arc to the north. Ivan's destructive path was now predicted to be along Barbados and Saint Vincent. This gave us an uncomfortable margin of less than 100 miles.

In the early morning we woke to discover that Ivan had increased to a Category 4 hurricane and the track was through the Grenadines and northern Grenada. A Category 4 hurricane has sustained winds of 131-155 mph. The

Quest vs. Ivan: A Heavyweight Match

National Oceanic and Atmospheric Administration (NOAA) describes the consequences of a Category 4 hurricane as 'complete roof structure failures on small residences. Shrubs, trees, and all signs are blown down. There is a very high risk of injury or death to people'. We were in for it. There was no where to run. We would make our stand on our boat in Clarkes Court Bay Marina. Ivan would come calling at 2:30 that afternoon. There wasn't a minute to lose. We had 48 hours of work to do in eight hours. We raced into town in the 4X4 to fuel up and buy any supplies that would be left on the shelves of the stores. When we reached Saint George I pulled into the first gas station. I expected the pumps to be out of fuel. Since there were no customers, I went into the office and asked if they were already out of fuel. The owner looked at me with his customary blank melancholy stare.

"Why would we be out of fuel?" he said.

"The hurricane" I said.

He laughed. "Grenada never get hit by hurricanes mon."

We filled up and I drove like a madman to the supermarket. The scene was surreal. It was a normal day in Paradise. The usual group of loafers milled about the entrance to the supermarket.

"There's a hurricane coming" I said.

They grinned. They laughed. A chorus of snickers followed us. Inside the store the staff and shoppers showed absolutely no concern about an approaching major hurricane. We tore up and down the aisles stuffing the cart with everything that our little Suzuki would hold and made it back to the marina by 9 AM.

The new track reported for Ivan was to pass directly over our location at 2:30 that afternoon. It was a strong Category 4 hurricane and building, and the ground speed was decreasing. Was this really happening? It seemed like a dream as we prepared Quest for the ride of our lives. All canvas was stowed, blades taken off the wind generator, bimini removed, halyards lashed to the mast, dinghy lashed on deck, docking lines doubled, etc. We worked in a blur for five hours. I looked up around noon to see two mini-vans pulling into the parking lot. One of the marina residents/winter cruisers came over to our boat and asked if we wanted a ride to the hotel.

"Ride to the hotel? No!" I said. "I'm a bit busy right now."

The only boaters that chose to stay and protect their boats were Wendy and I, a Canadian couple, a hired delivery captain from Victoria, Canada and the marina manager. Twenty or so boat owners had abandoned their boats to the most destructive forces of nature.

A description of the type of dock construction at Clarkes Court Bay Marina will give some idea of the crazy ride we were about to take. The marina consisted of two docks about one hundred feet long. Eight finger piers were spaced along each side of these main docks. The finger piers to which the boats were moored were about forty feet long. The entire marina was a floating dock system. The wooden planking for the docks rested on black plastic floats about two feet thick and about five by five feet square. The floats were secured to the bottom with screw anchors and criss-crossing chains. There were no pilings holding the docks in place. The system is designed and sold primarily to be used in small sheltered fresh water lakes in the mid west and Canada where there is no tide.

By 1 PM the entrance to Clarkes Court Bay was impassable. Ten foot white-crested breakers roared in from the ocean. This entrance is normally flat even under storm conditions. The skies turned a very threatening grey black and then a fine mist began to fall. We headed into the cabin and turned on the VHF and instruments. You could hear and feel the panic of the boaters on the VHF radio. The last official message from the government weather radio was that Ivan had increased to a Category 5 hurricane, 150 mph plus. The eye was predicted to pass several miles south of our location. Then the radio went silent. The government radio mast had blown away.

We were in the worst scenario possible, the north quadrant of a Category 5 hurricane. The recording barometer on board Quest had been dropping steadily since the morning. It now took a nose dive. It was well below 1000 millibars. The wind was up to 45 mph. I cooked a light lunch and then just waited. By 2:30 the wind was up to 60 mph and the docks were rocking so violently that no one would consider walking on them. By 3 PM the wind was holding steady at 90 mph. I mean steady. The wind anemometer seemed stuck at 90. I asked Wendy to get the manual for the instrument. Sure enough 90 mph was the maximum speed that could be displayed. The wind held above 90 mph for about an hour. Around 4:00 the wind dropped down to 60. Just around that time we heard a knocking on our deck. A knocking on the deck? I looked out the companionway and the marina manager was standing there buffeted by the storm.

"You had better get your rain gear and come with me, a boat broke loose" he said.

We jumped into our gear. I took one last look at the wind speed - 60 gusting to 65 mph. The barometer was in the ditch.

When we stepped out on the dock it was completely disorienting. The entire dock system, one hundred feet of main pier as well all the fingers, had shifted south 45 degrees and had been dragged a full hundred feet to the south west. This was really bad; the dock's anchors were not holding up to the force of the storm. There was no time to lose. We ran to the second dock to help secure the boat that was in danger. It took us about a half an hour to jury rig some dock lines on the distressed boat so that it wouldn't fly away when the wind freshened. Quick as we could, we returned to what we thought was the safety of Quest. Rain hitting skin at 60 mph felt like piercing needles. We were forced to walk sideways to make any progress. It was laborious to breathe. The docks were pitching so hard we had to crawl on our hands and knees back to Quest.

When we got back to the cabin the wind dropped to forty-five mph. Were we safe? Had the storm passed? No, we were passing through the eye of the hurricane. The barometer was now below 900 millibars. Was this possible? The wind previously had blown from due north. This meant that the island was blocking most of the force of the wind. The wind started to veer more southerly and pick up speed. Then the wind started to freshen straight from the south. Clarkes Court Bay opens to the south. We were now exposed to the full fury of Ivan. The monster that was being unleashed and about to hit us was beyond comprehension.

The wind built from the south for the next twenty minutes until the anemometer was again pegged at 90 mph and holding. Our situation had become much graver. We were exposed to the considerable ocean swells that were funneling up Clarkes Court Bay from the open sea. The docks were pitching like corks and taking us along for the ride. The rain started to fall in torrents. Looking out from the port lights there appeared one continuous wall of water. Visibility was less than five feet. The last two hours were just a warm up for what would happen next.

On the finger pier directly opposite Quest was a huge forty foot catamaran. On the next finger pier directly east of us was a very large heavy 45 foot aluminum luxury sailing yacht named Bella Brett. The anemometer was pegged at 90 mph. But judging from the deafening roar of the wind, it greatly exceeded 90. Wendy and I couldn't hear each other without screaming. We were no more than ten feet apart. As the wind built, the pitching and yawing became so intense that I needed to hold on to the saloon table just to keep from falling on the floor. During one of my most vivid memories I recall sitting down and staring at my hand. I remember an odd sense of calm. I felt like an observer, someone watching the events in a movie.

Then I heard Wendy scream "The cat is going to cut us in half!"

Quest and Crew

I crawled my way over to starboard. The sight from the port light was unbelievable. The catamaran's pontoons were about seven feet from top to bottom. Each time a swell hit the catamaran, the entire pontoon came out of the water. The pontoon climbed so high that the bottom was clearly visible. It was just a few feet from Quest. It looked just like a giant shear poised to chop us into bits.

At that moment we were given a very strong distraction to take our minds off the catamaran. We felt an incredible impact on the port side. Both Wendy and I were knocked to the floor. I got up and looked out the port hole. It appeared that the bow of Bella Brett, the sailboat on our port side, was trying to climb into Quest's cockpit. I ran to the companionway and threw the hatch open. The yacht's bow was jammed firm against the hull of Quest. Then in an instant, the yacht and her finger pier were gone. It was there one minute; then in the blink of an eye it was gone. The hurricane had blown boat and dock away like a feather.

A moment after Bella Brett disappeared into the storm, an incredibly loud smashing sound came from starboard. Although the scraping, grinding noise was deafening, we felt no impact to Quest. I looked out the port hole. The catamaran lines had stretched and its pontoons were now striking the center of the dock two feet from Quest. The dock was the only thing that separated us from the catamaran's rampage. It seemed certain that we were about to be destroyed by the catamaran.

Then we had a major bit of good fortune. As I watched the pontoon come closer and closer to Quest, knowing that it was just a matter of moments before it chopped us to bits, the dock flipped on its edge exposing the bottom of the dock floats to the starboard side of Quest. Under the strain of the increased tension of our dock lines, the forty-five foot dock cracked in the middle. The dock floats were pressed firmly against Quest cradling her from the catamaran. The wooden walkway of the dock was firmly affixed against the pontoon of the catamaran. Quest, the dock, and the catamaran were now knit together firmly by a spider web of dock lines.

Of greater concern was the fact that the finger pier to which we were moored had disengaged from the main dock. The catamaran, the finger pier, and Quest had loosed our terrestrial bonds. We were spinning out of control in a Category 5 hurricane. I turned on the GPS and ever so slightly we could see the latitude and longitude changing. The wind was gusting at 150 mph straight from the south. At least with that wind direction we wouldn't be blown to sea. We would be beached somewhere up in Clarkes Court Bay. All things considered this was a very consoling alternative.

We spun and sailed around Clarkes Court Bay for about thirty minutes. Every so often we would hear a very loud report. We assumed that the catamaran had again collided with some sort of floating object or debris. Although the ride was rough, Quest never made impact with anything. Then out of no where came the sustained grinding sound of a boat being grounded on rock. This sound from the depths of hell was the catamaran being beached and forced up on shore. We waited and anticipated that Quest also would be dragged up on the rocks. The minutes dragged on. We never even scraped the bottom. The catamaran was firmly beached and she wasn't moving.

An hour passed during which time we took a beating from the surge that was pounding Quest's hull from the windward side. The side of Quest was pointing south in the direction of wind and wave. Our lines held us fast to the overturned dock and the beached catamaran. After an hour the wind dropped to 60 mph. It is hard to imagine but 60 mph seems like a relative calm after a 155 mph hurricane. Then the wind slackened to 45 mph. The storm was passing. From the time that the dock had broken free to that moment, we hadn't looked out the port lights. There was no point. We couldn't have seen ten feet. We had no idea where we were. We could have been anywhere in Clarkes Court Bay.

"Do you hear a banging on the hull?" I asked Wendy.

Sure enough there was a knocking on the hull. I stuck my head out of the companionway into the gale. The marina manager was standing on our deck holding onto the shrouds with both hands.

"You two had enough fun?" he asked.

The catamaran was beached directly in front of the marina office. He had been watching us for the last thirty minutes.

"Do you want to come and spend the night in the office?"

I couldn't believe it; we were parked in front of the office. The office was of new construction and had been built with storms in mind. It hadn't blown away like every other building in Grenada. We threw on our wet gear, climbed over the broken dock and the catamaran, then jumped to dry land. The storm wasn't over but the hurricane had passed. It was as dark as midnight so we couldn't assess the damages to Quest. We feared the worst.

The storm continued to wail the entire night. We got very little sleep. I kept waking and forgetting where I was. We had lived on Quest for three years and during all that time we hadn't been away from her for more than a couple of nights. All the worst thoughts went through my mind. She must be in pretty bad shape. The dawn came. I forced myself to look out the office windows. Quest was floating fifty feet from the window like a prop in a tragic comedy. At a quick glance I couldn't see any damage. I ran out of the office and came up next to Quest. There wasn't a scratch on her port side. There was a bit of dock rash where she had rubbed the black rubber of the floats. I checked the port side. There was a scrape in the hull about halfway up the topsides where Bella Brett had struck her. There were a couple of pieces of teak trim missing. That was it. I climbed on board. There didn't appear to be any serious damage, none.

The marina was a complete write off. About half the boats were holed and had sunk. A quarter of the boats were beached. The entire docking system had broken up and been scattered everywhere by the hurricane. Even the boats that remained floating all had sustained serious damage. And then there was Quest floating almost pristine in the center of the carnage.

Grenada was completely destroyed. The hurricane

denuded every tree on the island. Grenada had gone from a lush tropical island to a desert in a few short hours. No more mangos, no more coconuts, no more bananas, mon. The island's infrastructure was gone: no power, water, communications, or planes. By 7:00 the next morning the looting began. The liquor stores and the rum shops were ransacked in the first hour. Then the food stores were looted. Happy with their supply of munchies and free rum, the drunken mob set out in a more random pattern of destruction and mayhem. The civil and military authorities were dispatched to protect the wealthy Grenadians and government officials. They kept off the streets entirely. There was not a uniform to be seen on the island.

The marina was in a lucky spot. It was situated in a rather remote part of the island. It wasn't until the fourth day that the looters developed any interest in us. They started by stripping the beached and abandoned boats at night. The more brazen looters wandered around by day swinging the ubiquitous machete. Seeing a volatile situation developing we cast off from the catamaran and anchored well off in the bay. This put us out of reach of the looters and thugs. The cruisers who were forced to protect their property lived with a constant tension and fear that the looters would become aggressive. This never came to pass. The looters and thieves had no stomach for a fight. They only took what was unprotected. After about a week we left our island home and sailed for Trinidad.

Visit www.questandcrew.com to view photographs of damage caused by Hurricane Ivan in Grenada

Two

A Funny thing happened on the way to buy a Boat

I was born and grew up in a small steel town on the Welland Canal in southern Ontario. As a young man I did not share the allure of working in a steel factory with my childhood friends. With familial and social pressures closing in from all sides, I left this cultural enclave when I was eighteen. After a successful attempt at higher education and a few dollars in my pocket, I set off to see the world. I had been traveling in the Mediterranean and Middle East for six months when I met my future wife in the old city of Jerusalem. We immediately fell hopelessly in love. I now had a friend, lover and traveling companion to share my travels and sometimes laugh at my bad jokes.

We traveled to Egypt and devoted our lives to each other at the Pyramids in Giza. It was an informal ceremony for two at the top of the Great Pyramid. The joyous occasion was brought to a sudden conclusion by protests from the army personnel guarding the antiquity. We would be arrested if we didn't come down immediately. In our exuberance we had failed to read and comprehend the signs that were posted plainly in all languages to stay off the pyramids under penalty of law. After being dragged from the last levels of stone by two burly and quite furious guards, I explained to them that I had just proposed to Wendy. A momentary mild form of sentimentality got the better of their judgment. We were not arrested. For almost thirty years we have been at each other's sides.

About twelve years ago, my wife and I purchased a Bayfield 36 sailboat. We were smitten with the dream of becoming 'Caribbean Cruisers'. Before our purchase of Quest, my sailing and boating experience could be aptly described by one word: none. I had no boating experience; practical, theoretical or otherwise. As a child I had spent many a warm afternoon daydreaming on the banks of the Welland Canal watching the huge steamers passing by. This gave a naïve child all the information needed to understand boating. In my young adolescent mind a boat was a means to transport coal, iron ore, and timber from source to factory. My father's four brothers earned their livelihood as merchant seamen on the Great Lakes. Traveling as an occasional guest on their merchant ships as they transited the Welland canal and locks from Lake Ontario to Lake Erie further underscored the utilitarian nature of boating. I believe that the good people of Welland knew of the concept of 'Yachting'. It just didn't happen in Welland.

For these many reasons it came as a complete surprise to my wife when I called her at work in the fall of 1998 with the crazy idea of buying a cruising boat. She was well aware that sailing was a skill that I did not possess. It came as an even bigger surprise to me when I eventually wore her down and she agreed to the plan.

A Funny thing happened on the way to buy a Boat

Wendy and I were living in the outer fringe of Charlotte, North Carolina. Many of our neighbors had a biblical outlook on life and worldly events. They were right wing Christian extremists. Combining bad science, God and guns they had embraced the Y2K madness and all of its impending doom theory with fervor. The threat of apocalypse suited their lifestyle. One of our heavily armed and dangerous neighbors who had fallen for the Y2K hoax came over to my house. He requested that I drop whatever I was doing and research a rather arcane point about Ford trucks.

"I've got to know when Ford started to put computer chips in the F250 trucks" he said. "You know how to work those PC things."

While searching for a definitive answer, my searches strayed to an article entitled 'Cruise the Caribbean on a sailboat for $15,000 a year'. I was shocked to discover that people lived on sailboats year round. I was surprised that it could be done so cheaply. I was trapped. After an hour discovering the world of full-time liveaboard cruisers I couldn't understand why everyone didn't buy a boat. I had to get this plan going fast before all the good boats were bought up.

It was time to take a leadership role with Wendy. I came at her with a strong approach to what I knew would be serious opposition. I called Wendy at work.

"Hi honey" I said. "Did you know that people can cruise the Caribbean in sailboats for about $15,000 a year?"

"FORGET IT, FORGET IT, FORGET IT..."

Wow, this was serious opposition. Seeing no

window of opportunity, I hung up. I called back in ten minutes.

"Forget it, forget it… You don't know how to sail… I'm afraid of drowning…"

Wendy voiced strong reservations. She obviously didn't possess my highly advanced level of new-found acumen on the subject of live aboard cruising.

"Just listen to me for twenty minutes" I said.

"Ten minutes is all you've got. I have to go to a meeting" she replied.

This was the ten minutes that changed our lives.

My ten minute pitch included some dubiously embellished facts with a little blue water, warm sandy beaches and sunsets thrown in for dramatic effect. Two hours after I had read the first article on cruising the whole idea was really starting to sound possible. I was even starting to believe it myself.

"OK, tell me more when I get home" she said.

By 9 PM that night, the polls were split between 'this is crazy - definitely the most hair brained idea that you have ever had' to 'maybe we could do it'. By the weekend, the seed had sprouted and put out healthy roots. For a week, I concentrated my research on what would be the perfect cruising boat for a couple who had never set foot on a sailboat. Wendy and I trolled the local bookstores for books on cruising. All the helpful information in print and on the Web pointed to a 36 - 40 foot heavy blue water boat. Further searches revealed the usual list of suspects: Cabo Rico, Hans Christian, Pacific Seacraft, Island Packet. These are boats that even a complete novice can't sink in a gale. I

A Funny thing happened on the way to buy a Boat

knew the type and size of boat. It was just a matter of finding a good yacht broker. Charlotte, North Carolina was not the right place to look for an agent.

The following Monday I contacted a broker in Annapolis, Maryland. Within a week, the broker had compiled a list of boats that were in imminent danger of being bought by Wendy and me. The best selection of boats for sale in the winter was in Fort Lauderdale, Florida. On the broker's five page printout for our Fort Lauderdale trip were about a hundred boats. I highlighted three Cabo Ricos, two Hans Christians, an Allied Princess, and two Pacific Seacrafts, all of which looked promising. Almost overlooked on the list was a Bayfield 36.

"What about this Bayfield 36?" I asked the broker. "Is this a power boat?"

"No, it's not a Bayliner. It's a beautiful boat with classic lines" he said. "They really hold their value. They were made in Ontario, Canada - fine workmanship, solid blue water boat. You should definitely see it."

It went on the list of boats to see.

A month to that auspicious day that I first phoned Wendy with plans to completely restructure our lives, we traveled to Fort Lauderdale on a boat buying mission filled with hope and expectation. The morning after we arrived, we set out early with a local broker to narrow the list. The broker's story never changed. Within two blocks of every prospective dream boat and without a hint of subterfuge, the broker would look at me and say "This one is pristine... This one is bristol."

After six wasted hours in the heat of the Florida

sun crawling over these neglected broken boats we were losing our momentum. I started to believe that all old boats smelled like a locker room and had three inches of oil in the bilge. We had visited eight boats. I was tired. I wanted a beer. We had just one boat left. Should we even bother? Fort Lauderdale is without doubt the land of many tired boats. It was getting late in the afternoon and the broker was pushing us to see the Bayfield 36 named Quest. It was docked in a canal behind a house two blocks from the downtown area of Fort Lauderdale. When we rounded the house and saw Quest, it was love at first sight.

Wendy pulled me aside and said "This is it."

A Bayfield 36 is a unique combination of new and old with her beautiful clipper bow, trail boards, and teak combings. This is a "big" 36-footer with classic lines that would not be out of place in a pirate movie. We did a walk through. She was pristine.

"Do you want her?" I asked Wendy.

"Let's buy it" she said.

I told the broker to set up a haul for the next weekend. Our broker in Annapolis would find the surveyor to thoroughly examine all the systems of the boat. The haul and survey were set up for the next Saturday. Every thing was falling into place, with the exception of one small but critical detail. When we got home, we realized that we had scheduled the survey for Super Bowl Sunday. I couldn't beg, borrow or steal a hotel room in Fort Lauderdale. It didn't go over well when I asked the selling broker in Miami if we could stay on the boat Saturday and Sunday. I knew there wasn't much chance of him letting us stay overnight on her.

A Funny thing happened on the way to buy a Boat

This idea was worse than having someone interested in buying your house move in and become a house guest for a couple of weeks. I called my broker in Annapolis who smoothed out the troubled waters. I received a 'thumbs up' to stay on the boat for the two nights. We arrived that Saturday. Fort Lauderdale was overrun with Super Bowl fever. We were moored far away from the revelers. We enjoyed a perfect evening and quiet night aboard Quest.

A boat survey - this was going to be fun, right? Surveys are lengthy, slow, meticulous, and gruelingly boring. We started very early around 7:00 in the morning. By 2 PM, the surveyor had crawled through the bilge, climbed to the top of the mast, turned everything on and tested all the gear. The sea trial was the only part of the survey remaining. Ah, a 'sea trial', how romantic! It went over my head when the surveyor warned me that the Gulf Stream was close in, the wind was howling at 25 knots gusting to 30 north by northwest, and the sea was 15 feet and confused. His further advice that we stay in the protected water of the Intracoastal Waterway went over my head as well.

"This is a blue water boat, isn't it? Why can't we take it out on the ocean?" I asked.

He shrugged. From the marina to the ocean was about three miles and three bridge openings. Wendy and I lounged in the tropical sun on the foredeck while the salesman motored up the canal. We hit the cut at the Port of Fort Lauderdale about an hour later and raised the main and jib. This was great - my first time on a sail boat, my first time on the ocean. By the time we got a half mile into the

Gulf Stream, the ocean started to look pretty scary. The boat was plunging into troughs and climbing peaks like a roller coaster ride. Ten minutes later, it felt like we were in a washing machine. I became queasy, then completely disoriented. I was experiencing an overdose of 'mal de mare'. I was nauseous. I had cold sweats. My fingers and toes went numb. I was losing consciousness. I was not a pillar of strength. Seconds before I passed out, I told the surveyor to get us back to the boatyard. The rest of the sea trial was a confusing dream. I regained a modicum of consciousness when we were back in the calm waters of the Fort Lauderdale canals. I had never felt worse but I was occasionally coherent. After what felt like days we tied off at our assigned slip at Summerfield's Marina in the bowels of Fort Lauderdale. I staggered over the gunwales of Quest and threw up against a palm tree.

After wiping my face on my sleeve, I walked over to the broker and said "Good boat, we'll take her."

Perhaps it was stubbornness or pride; perhaps it was the fact that I just didn't want our tropical dream to disappear. For whatever reason Quest would be ours.

The story of how we came to purchase Quest would end if it were not for the bank robbery. When we got home, I had a check certified and couriered to my broker in Annapolis. As the broker had done hundreds of times before, he walked across the street to his bank to deposit the check into an escrow account. While he was standing at the counter waiting his turn in line, he unknowingly dropped the deposit slip and check on the floor. While he was waiting in line, two masked armed men

A Funny thing happened on the way to buy a Boat

came through the door.

"Everyone put your hands up and don't move" one of the robbers shouted.

One of the thieves jumped the counter while his accomplice stood guard with a sawed off shot gun. The incident was over and the robbers were out of the bank in less than five minutes. The headline from the Annapolis Capital daily newspaper for February 18, 1999 reads 'Robbers strike Eastport bank'. My broker Bill was frozen to the spot during the entire robbery. As the robbers exited the bank, Bill noticed the check and deposit slip under his heel and thoughtfully pocketed both. The police arrived a few minutes later and sealed off the bank.

"Don't touch anything" the officer ordered.

The staff and the customers were detained an hour for questioning. Bill was finally allowed to leave. He returned to his office across the street and immediately phoned me.

"You're not going to believe what just happened" he said. "I was in the bank depositing your check and the bank got robbed."

My heart sank. If the check had been taken away in the booty it would take weeks to straighten out.

"So they got the check?" I asked forlornly.

"No. It was stuck to the bottom of my shoe the whole time during the robbery" he said. "As soon as the bank reopens it will be deposited."

The following day Bill deposited the earnest money into the escrow account and it was wired to the Fort Lauderdale broker.

Quest and Crew

Buying a 20,000 pound blue water cruising boat proved to be relatively quick and easy. Now what do we do? The skeleton of a plan was to have Quest trucked to our house outside Charlotte and set up on the hard for a complete overhaul. She was in very good shape as twenty year old boats go. The harsh conditions of the tropics had taken away her gleam and the instruments were obsolete. Our future dreams included mooring in the most remote anchorages and being completely self-sufficient. Quest may have been ready for ocean cruising twenty years ago. Technologies that were unheard of when she came out of the mold in 1986 were now commonplace. Solar panels, wind generators and inverter would power an array of high tech gadgets, instruments and a good sized refrigerator. Our joy and pride in ownership led us to explore possible new acquisitions to upgrade Quest. At times it was startling to see the exorbitant price tags of marine gear.

With complete faith in our future and no concern for failure, we strove to develop our plans for where we would sail Quest and how we would equip her. She may have been just another old boat but every thing about Quest was new to us. Even the language of boating with its arcane terminology would dominate our conversations for the next years. However, the skills that were prerequisite to become competent sailors on an unforgiving sea would need to wait. Charlotte was a long way from the ocean. We had just begun the process of investing our lives, hopes and dreams into a new journey. In all respects that is how Wendy and I met and it is how we have spent our lives together these many years.

Three

A Two Ton Paperweight

What do you do when you buy a 20,000 pound paperweight? You buy something solid to put under it: 20,000 lbs of gravel ought to work. Quest had a very distinctive classic look on the water. She also looked quite striking when she was laid on the hard in the woods beside our house. A full dump truck load of gravel became the first item in what became an endless list of invoices. Quest became a local landmark beside our house on February 19th 1999. Two hundred and fifty miles from the nearest ocean she was out of her element. The trucker backed his split bed rig onto the freshly smoothed out gravel. He gently lowered Quest. He set up and tightened the boat stands. Then he was gone. Quest and I began a partnership that would last seven years. Quest and her crew would some day travel to many foreign places. But being beached in Charlotte in a forest with snow on the ground must have seemed the most foreign to her.

My first official duty for the next week was to explain to the resident gawkers what a forty foot sailboat was doing beside my house. My first encounter with the locals was not inspired. I must admit that my answers to their questions lacked definition. The repetitive nature of the inquiries gave me sufficient practice to hone appropriately evasive answers. I had to do something. I was now a representative of the cruiser lifestyle. I was a cruiser wannabe with a boat. For the sake of neighborly harmony, I dodged direct questions and concentrated on being vague. After all interested parties received their tour of Quest and were assured that their property values wouldn't plummet, the multitudes departed with quizzical expressions on their faces.

My first month of boat ownership was a completely cerebral experience. The weather that winter was exceptionally cold and icy. On my infrequent trips to the frozen decks of Quest it was icy enough to slide from bow to stern. Although skating on the decks of your boat could have a daring appeal to some, I opted instead to dive head first into our newly acquired pile of nautical reference books that lay in a heap on the living room floor. I read Tom Neale's book 'All in the Same Boat', then Nigel Calder's 'Manual of Mechanical and Electrical Systems'. Many others followed. In a month the weather moderated. The ice melted. It was time to get physical. I remember boarding Quest after my winter sojourn and sitting down in the saloon. Ahhh…it was great to luxuriate in the splendor of one's sailing yacht.

Where do you begin when you don't know how to begin? The survey was filed in one of the lockers. It was an 8 hour and 30 page marine survey. It should have some clues where to start. Except for the normal amount of wear for an old boat in the Caribbean, Quest had fared very well.

A Two Ton Paperweight

Wait a minute. Here's something in the comment section: 'odor permeating from sources unknown in the vicinity of the mast and head'. Sure enough, there was a smell. Quest had been closed up for a couple of months in the winter. If frozen waste smelled this bad, I could just imagine what it would smell like in the Charlotte summer at 100 degrees and 100% humidity.

I had my first project. It seemed prudent to get this one fixed before the co-owner got wind of it. I gathered the tools and began disassembling the head. Even with the floor bolts removed, the head refused to budge. I grabbed the bowl and gave it a good wrenching twist. The porcelain broke in two. It would have been much easier to remove the head in two halves if it were not for the sludge that dripped on the cabin floor. As I extricated the broken head and threw it overboard, it leaked an odiferous trail the entire length of the cabin sole. The situation quickly went from bad to worse. With the head gone, the open hoses were exposed. The full intensity of a waste system that had been closed for the past 25 years was now venting. It was time to do the manly thing. I opened the hatches and hit the road.

When I climbed down the ladder, the fresh air nudged my common sense. 'I better get rid of the evidence.' I loaded the busted head parts into a wheelbarrow and buried them in a distant corner of the property. After I finished covering the grave with some leaves to further disguise my intentions, I turned around to see my friend Junior sitting on a stump 25 feet behind me drinking a beer. He had a grin from ear to ear.

"I hope you don't mind, I went and took one of

your beers. What you got buried in that grave?"

"Nothing" I said.

In a situation this preposterous saying 'nothing' invited further scrutiny. Junior was a warm, honest person; he had spent four memorable years on battleships in the Pacific during the Vietnam War. I could tell him the truth.

"I had to bury some old greasy rags" I said.

"No you didn't" he said. "I've been sitting on that stump over there for the last thirty minutes. You weren't burying rags."

"OK, OK. I busted the head and I'm burying it so that it won't contaminate the side yard. And by the way, if you've been sitting there for 30 minutes, how many beers did you take out of my refrigerator?"

"Just one" he said. At least I wasn't the only one lying. "Don't change the subject, Dave. Contamination! You're worried that Wendy will see the broken shitter before you can fix it, right?" We both laughed at the complete absurdity of the situation. "Let's go on board. Show me what you messed up" he said.

"It's pungent in there" I replied.

"Did you find a dead body under the floor boards?" he asked."

When Junior came on board and saw the mess, he said "You're going to need a new head, boy." This was classic wry southern wit. "While you're at it, pull out all that ten feet of stinking waste hose. We have to take out that waste tank so you can clean it properly."

Junior demonstrated a definite knack around waste systems. We pulled up the floor boards and exposed the top of the waste tank.

"A twenty-five gallon waste tank! Some people don't like to throw out anything" Junior joked. He was right. For a boat our size it was enormous. "You could clean it out and make a second diesel tank" Junior said.

This guy was really thinking. We disconnected the vent and feed hose and started pulling up on the tank. It wasn't just tight, it seemed like it was cemented into the bottom of the bilge.

"We have to loosen it with 2x4's" Junior said. He jumped off Quest and sawed a ten foot 2x4 in half. "This will definitely work" he said.

We jammed the 2x4s between the side of the tank and the bilge walls. We started to rock back and forth in unison. After about three minutes, we heard a great cracking sound.

"See, I told you. That's all we needed to do" Junior said.

We both grabbed an end of the tank and gave a great heave upward. Without knowing it, the over aggressive prying had broken off the top of the tank. We pulled the top half of the tank up in one piece. The tank was so rotten that it had corroded on all four sides about six inches up from the bottom. We had the top of the tank in our hands and the bottom was in the bilge. The bottom contained about four inches of rich compost.

"I don't think that you're going to be able to make this into a diesel tank" Junior deadpanned.

"Can you help me get this mess out of here?" I asked.

We slung the top of the tank over the rail of the cockpit and bucketed out the greasy residue in the bottom of the tank. After a few beers and some deadly jokes, we managed to pry out the bottom of the tank and threw into the woods.

"You might want to bury it" Junior said. "It could be contaminated."

We were in the thick of it now. Our course was set. End to end with the waste tank in the bilge was the 25 gallon diesel tank. It had been emptied for the trip up from Florida so it would be a breeze to pull it out and clean it. We had complete success in pulling the diesel tank. We did make one unwanted discovery. When we got the diesel tank out of the boat and turned it over, it was also badly corroded to the extent that rendered it dangerous. The aluminum had rotted to a point that you could jam a screw driver right through the side. Right about then Junior's volunteering on boat projects came to a conclusion. He wouldn't be back on the boat for over a year.

What a day so far! A lot of boat refitting is unpleasant but dealing with the waste system is unique. The process evokes concerns of health dangers. I dragged the tank to the back of the yard where it could keep company with the buried head. The only job left was the cleanup. This shouldn't be tough. I'll spray the bilge down with the garden hose. I would need to hose down an area from the head to the diesel engine and then empty it out with the bilge pump. This is a good example of where a theory can come into direct conflict with the limitations of technology. Let's say that the bilge pump was undersized. Let's say that the lines were undersized. The system was adequate to handle drips from a leaking propeller shaft seal. It was not up to the task of pumping a bilge full of slime and chunks the size of my little finger. I started the pump and the slurry started to squirt from the through-hull at the back of the stern. After approximately one minute, the squirt became a drool. I cleaned out the intake. It squirted for a minute then drooled again down the topsides of Quest. The Bayfield is molded in such a way that the bilge empties into a huge sump right under the engine. The sump has a capacity of about 20 gallons. To get to the bilge opening is very difficult. The engine blocks any real access. But with the tanks missing, I could get at it from the saloon area. I needed a bucket and some line. I was half way down the boarding ladder when Wendy came home. I was covered in bilge goo. Think quickly!

I smiled and said "Hurry, change your clothes and give me some help."

"Don't you know what day it is?" she asked.

"I don't know… It's Wednesday or Thursday?"

"NO, IT'S MY BIRTHDAY!"

"I forgot again. Put some old clothes on, we've got work to do. No time for personal issues, the boat's got a BIG problem. Get changed and come on the boat."

Within half an hour, we had formed a bucket line and were making good progress. Every time I handed Wendy a bucket of slop, I said "Happy birthday!" I got the deep freeze on the first ten buckets. Then she started to thaw. By bucket twenty-five, we were both laughing. We worked by the light of an extension cord until 7 PM. Then

I received divine inspiration. Drill a hole through the side of the boat way below the water line. Theory was turned into action. I drilled a one inch hole through the outside of the hull which intersected the bottom of the bilge. No more slop buckets. I could now simply spray the bilge with the hose and let the wash exit through the hole in the side of the hull. Days of work were still ahead just to get the bilge clean enough before I could get into it without gagging, but not tonight.

Log: Day One: The retrofit of Quest has begun.

"So what happened today?" Wendy asked.

"It was the head's fault! Then Junior came over… and then the 2x4's. Then it got really bad." I was making no sense but I had all the excuses. "Wendy, this boat is over twenty five years old" I said

"So what does that mean?"

"Every system has to be verified."

What began as a peaceful morning had evolved into a serious project.

"I thought that you were just going to polish the teak."

"Hey that's the good news. The teak looks great and the head won't talk from the grave."

When you're on the hard, the current is always in your favor. Today's events marked a change in wind and tide for Quest and us. No longer could we afford the luxury of using our inexperience as an excuse. I had faith I could learn to sail. If we were going sailing without experience I needed to have a boat I could depend on. Today caught me off guard. If two inexperienced rookies were going to survive at sea we had to count on Quest being in perfect shape. This was the reality in paradise.

The broken head set off a cascade of destruction and retrofitting that would seem to never end. I would become overly familiar with the bilge over the next few weeks. The Bayfield 36 has a very long, wide, and deep bilge. At the stern and under the engine the bilge drops into a sump that is an additional two feet deep, two feet wide, and tapers down to a few inches at the end. The sump was the size of a small coffin and would provide the stage for one of the most terrifying moments of my entire life.

After I had scrubbed the bilge with degreaser, I deglazed the enamel paint with solvent. It was time to slop a few coats of bilge paint on. I decided to start by painting the tight coffin shaped sump section at the stern under the engine. Pot in left hand, brush in right, I crawled into the bilge, then under the engine. Another squeeze and I was down in the sump. The area was well lighted. It didn't look that tight. The only way that I could manage to get to the tapered end of the sump was to place my left arm at my side and extend my painting arm fully in front of me. I was about three inches from reaching the end with the wet brush. So close. Should I go and get something to extend my reach? No, that would take five extra minutes. I was completely focused on painting those elusive couple of inches at the end of the sump. I breathed out and forcefully pushed forward against the back of the sump with my feet. I jammed my body into a smooth four-sided funnel.

The moment I realized that I was stuck in the sump I didn't panic. I had actually reached the end of the bilge with the paintbrush. I had to finish the job. I tried to move back. I couldn't budge. I had never been in a situation where I was trapped. I have never shown any tendency toward claustrophobia. I actually like small tight spaces. My affinity for close spaces delayed the terror. But when the terror came, it enveloped me. I knew that I was being irrational. But on the other hand, I knew that I was going to die. My chest and back were jammed tight against the sides of the bilge. Scream? Forget it. I couldn't inhale enough air to get out a good expletive. My face was one foot from the paint pot. I'm going to suffocate on paint fumes. 'Local man dies in boating accident in side yard!' 'Boater drowns in bilge paint!' I was trapped and seconds felt like minutes.

This situation had a surprisingly simple resolution. I was wearing myself out from fear. My mind drifted to the time when Wendy would come home and find me stuck in the bilge. I laughed inwardly. After awhile I started to give in and accept the problem. 'I may be in this cramped position for six hours or more' I thought. I began to loosen up. That's when the walls of my coffin seemed to enlarge. Relaxing was the answer. I consciously relaxed my muscles starting with my feet, then up to my waist. After sufficient inhalation of paint solvents, my breathing slowed down and I was ready for a nap. While relatively intoxicated on bilge paint, I started wiggling backward millimeter by millimeter. I finally wiggled myself free.

I sat in a cramped ball in the bilge. I jumped into the cockpit and tried to loosen up. It was mid morning now. Sitting in the cockpit in the sunlight I really needed someone to have a good laugh with over this misstep. But there was nobody there. I never felt more alone in my life. I shook off the melancholy and continued my paint job with a paint brush duct-taped to the handle of a mop.

The simple task of ripping out tanks and refurbishing the bilge stretched on for months. This was the easy stuff. But I had begun the first step in the refitting of Quest. Eventually every system in Quest would be replaced with state-of-the-art equipment.

Four

After the Hurricane: Welcome to Trinidad

Eleven days after hurricane Ivan, Grenada showed little improvement. The devastation from the hurricane was complete. The entire population of Grenada had been traumatized. With the infrastructure destroyed, the country depended on foreign sources of food and water for its day to day survival. The civil and military authority had their hands full dealing with a shocked and unruly citizenry. Protection for a few hundred foreign sailors was out of the question. It was to our regret that we left Grenada September 18, 2004.

As we passed through the reef off Hog Island, our perspective on Grenada widened so that we had a grand vista of the south coast. The destroyed houses and anguished population were no longer in fine focus. A beautiful green land stripped of every leaf was our last memory of Grenada. We set our sails, our heading was due south. Our destination was the island of Trinidad.

After a brisk uneventful night sail, we were becalmed at sunrise. Our afternoon departure from Grenada put us five miles outside the Boca in the early morning. The Boca de Monos is the cut on the northern coast of Trinidad between the mainland and Monos Island that gives access to the Gulf of Paria. We were motoring in a slick sea when I first spotted the leading edge of the flotsam. It was early morning. Wendy and I were wide awake for our approach to Trinidad. We were sitting in the cockpit when a few plastic bottles floated by. Then there were a few more. I went to the bow.

"Wendy you've got to see this."

The morning light was obliquely striking a calm sea, outlining the spectacle.

"What is it?"

"It looks like a big dump from a garbage barge. It just seems a little close to the coast. Keep an eye on the intakes!"

This objectionable environmental oddity of floating plastic and refined petrochemicals served as our introduction to Trinidad. The bulk of the flotilla consisted primarily of empty plastic water bottles, fast food clam shell boxes, and plastic grocery bags. Trinidad practiced the medieval method of throwing one's refuse into the nearest ditch. Thank you, noble ancestors. The advantage of such an approach lies in its simplicity. The next big storm flushes the trash-clogged ditches into the bay; the next ebb tide sends the trash straight to the ocean, never to return.

The ability of this system to work efficiently lies in the delicate balance between the size of ditch, torrential rains, and the volume of trash. Trinidad has plenty of trash. The ditches were enormous. The rain could always be counted upon. First world countries prefer to collect their trash and heap it into mountains later to be stylized into golf courses. Alas, Trinidad's golf community was small. Cricket and soccer were the big draws. The golf community simply didn't have the membership base to make the dream of whacking the round, dimpled ball around a refurbished refuse facility financially practical. So out to the sea went the garbage and, with it, several potential golf courses a year.

After our night sail from Grenada, this wasn't the kind of welcome I would add to a tourist brochure. However, this unwanted introduction to Trinidad served as a proper warning. We didn't know it at the time but Trinidad would become our beloved home for the next year and a half. We grew to love Trinidad for what she is and we would ignore her foibles.

We put the mainland to our left and Monos Island to our right and motored straight through the Boca. The safety of Chaguaramas lay only five miles further. We were both still feeling the residual shock of the hurricane. We hadn't died. We hadn't fallen apart. We were psychologically tempered. This gave us the edge we needed to deal with the sights and sounds of Chaguaramas. You can be warned. We were warned. But we were now experiencing the stories of Chaguaramas in real time.

Chaguaramas is a multi-use harbor. It was still hurricane season so Chaguaramas had more boats on the dry than all the yards in the Caribbean combined. Trinidad also has a thriving off shore oil exploration industry. So a good part of Chaguaramas is set aside for servicing oil rigs. Even the Trinidad Coast Guard had its main base in Chaguaramas. There were dry docks for medium sized ships. There was even a large fishing and smuggling village. All this was squeezed into two miles of waterfront.

The anchorage itself was no less diverse, with fishing boats from China, propane tankers from Canada, bauxite ore carriers, and service boats of every description. Amongst this heavy industry, pleasure boats eked out their small space. To an unaccustomed eye, it was bedlam. However, 'chaos' should be reserved to describe the complete disregard for the basic rules of boating in the harbor. Everyone had the right of way, all of the time. Size of vessel was the sole legitimizer of all marine maneuvers. An approaching boat might pass on the right or the left or they might choose to make circles around you at high speed if something shiny caught their eye. It was a Bowditch nightmare. Compliance to rules was completely discretionary. Speed limits in the harbor were only limited by maximum hull speed. Chaguaramas was the Dodge City of boating, Water World come to life.

"Quest, this is Cayenne III, come in."

I looked at Wendy and said "They're calling another Quest."

"Cayenne III to Quest, come in. We have been watching your approach."

Who is Cayenne III and why would they be watching us? I called back to Cayenne "Quest here."

"We've been expecting you for a couple of hours."

"Well, we would have been here sooner but we had to motor through a mountain of garbage in the Boca."

After a long night of sailing the laughter coming from their open mike was inviting.

Within ten minutes we were surrounded by bobbing dinghies. Everyone wanted to personally greet us and they wanted news of Grenada. We were not going to slip quietly into Trinidad. This is how fast you can lose your anonymity. Grenada was still in a communication blackout so the only news received in Trinidad was from cruisers who had sailed south after the hurricane. This 'instant celebrity' status buoyed us. It also entitled us to one free night at the Customs dock and immediate haul-out at one of the many boatyards the next day. Trinidadians and the boating community have very big hearts. They were watching the developments in Grenada with great interest. There probably wasn't a person on the island, citizen or foreign cruiser, that didn't have a friend in Grenada and they all wanted to get in touch with them.

I expected problems in Paradise. That's Trinidad. Everyone personally warned us before we sailed for Trinidad, even people we had never met, even people who had never been to Trinidad! There are countries where I have traveled that I can remember vaguely. There are countries that I wish to forget. Trinidad made a lasting, treasured impression.

Trinidad is a country of extremes. It is one of the warmest, friendliest places on the planet. Trinidad also has one of the highest murder rates in the world. This fact carries with it a level of status. It engenders fear and at the same time a particular pride among the population. The population is split socially and racially between Blacks and Hindus. They meet for commerce. They intermarry. But largely they stay apart, with the Blacks in the north and the

Hindus in the south. In ordinary conversation, both populations dwell on the subject of racism. They argue about it. They debate it constantly. This obsession and obscure discussions of whether someone is half black or a quarter Hindu could only take place in Trinidad. Trinidad embraces complete social openness. Common conversations that would be taboo and beyond the pale of political correctness anywhere else are just food for thought in Trinidad.

For the repair and storage of boats, Chaguaramas has no equal. You can take on any marine repair with the confidence that you can find the product and the labor to accomplish it. The availability of well-priced product and cheap capable labor all within two miles dovetails with a laissez faire attitude toward basic environmental risks. This combination removes a great deal of the burden when dealing with the more toxic aspects of boat maintenance and repair.

Chaguaramas reflects the tremendous contrasts that are a hallmark of Trinidad society. The same paint job could cost you $1000 or it could cost you $10,000. A boat owner paying the high end would naturally get complete turn key service, a project manager who spoke any language you wish (French, German, English), an estimate, a bill, a guarantee of sorts, but most importantly a feeling that everything was right with the world. But what the boat owner contracting for the full service plan seldom realizes is that the job, regardless of the cost, will be performed by the same laborers, using exactly the same product, in somewhat different manners, under somewhat different conditions, as the low-end job. These scales of service in themselves would not be a revelation if it were not for the fact that high-end turnkey jobs frequently fail due to insufficient attention to detail. In most cases, the failure isn't discovered until the boater is a long way from Chaguaramas.

The reputation that Trinidad has earned in the boat service industry is a result of cultural norms and practices. Swiss trains run on time. Paint in Trinidad was mixed in discarded soda bottles. The handful of families that hold the reins of power in Chaguaramas want every job to be perfect. But if the quality of services were brought up to the standards of a first world country, then the prices would follow. Who would go to Chaguaramas if the prices were equal to or higher than the prices in Miami? My description, albeit an over-simplified view, has an even more over-simplified solution. If you haul a boat in Chaguaramas, do the work yourself and hire semi-skilled labor to help you.

Wendy and I came to Chaguaramas by accident. The accident's name was Ivan. Unlike the far majority of sailboats in Grenada after hurricane Ivan, Quest was very much sea worthy. Quest was unharmed. We made our way to Trinidad simply to paint the bottom and replace a ten foot section of teak rail that had gone missing in the storm. A job that should have taken two weeks stretched into a year and a half. This wasn't necessarily a case of extreme procrastination. It was just another example of the age old phenomenon of project creep. This is the same dynamic that begins with wiping a smudge off a window, which causes the cleaning of the window, which causes the cleaning of all the windows in the house, which then leads to the full house paint job.

Despite the overwhelming number of boats in the yards of Chaguaramas, no one hauls unnoticed in this two mile stretch of boat works. By the time that the boat stands are screwed tight, you, your boat and your wallet have been analyzed by the seemingly casual expert glances of a dozen or so contractors. For one fleeting moment you become the center of their collective attention. Years of experience dictate the ceremonial carving of a first time Chaguaramas visitor. Within one hour, all the various contractors' differences have been put aside. A plan is established by their consensual agreement. We now belonged to Garth.

Over the next year and a half, Garth would become our friend and enemy. These two opposing states could and would happen on the same day. To keep us properly entertained, Garth brought in his full crew. This platoon of larcenous angels included his half brother Denzel and his other half brother Calvin. They were the nucleus of the atom.

Around this nucleus orbited the rest of the organization, the 'five others'. The 'five others' were normally shoeless, shirtless and opinionless. They strove to maintain invisible personas. They were the disenfranchised.

We had contracted Garth to paint the boot stripe and the two foot wide stripe about half the way up the top sides. Garth's paint jobs had the regularity of a ceremony. They began and ended… in a trash barrel. When the surface to be painted had been prepped and taped, Garth barked orders to his crew.

"Time to paint! You, you go paint shack."

Off he runs. Simultaneously, his brother Denzel locates the closest trash barrel. He rummages and locates an appropriate mixing container for the paint. With skill borne of practice, he cuts the top off the plastic bottle with a box cutter and drizzles the residual sticky contents onto the ground. He waves the half bottle in the air with great flair, assuring Garth and all observers that in fact the container is clean and pristine.

"Garth, what's the soda bottle for?" I asked.

"Mon, that's the mixing pot."

At that moment, Garth was bracing for combat and not in a conversational mood. He was an actor and magician preparing for his stage act. 'The other' returns with the paint. The compressor is started. Garth pulls his paint gun from his lunch bag. He removes his tee shirt and wraps it around his mouth, transforming his 'Fruit of the Loom' into a low-tech and absolutely useless paint respirator.

Things are moving fast now. Half-brother Denzel opens the paint and the paint catalyst and double free-hand pours into the pop bottle. One hundred years of paint chemistry reduced to the art of a bartender mixing a gin martini. While Garth mounts the scaffolding, Denzel fills the paint sprayer, attaches the air line, and tosses it up to Garth. I am horrified. It all happened too fast and with such momentum that no one responded to my protests except Wendy.

Five coats of primer were applied in fifteen minutes. Fifteen minutes more and the poly wrap protecting the rest of the boat from overspray was pulled away along with the masking tape and thrown in the trash barrel. Just as advertised, a Garth paint job, trash barrel to trash barrel in thirty minutes or less. Garth unknotted his tee shirt respirator and placed it on his shoulders. One of 'the others' handed him a rum bottle. Taking a good swallow of 180 proof to inoculate him from the paint fumes, he beamed.

"Beautiful job mon."

I looked down and shook my head. Garth could set a speed record for painting a 40 foot boat. It was an utter mess.

"Don't worry mon, this is how we do it in Chaggy."

The 'five others' then spent two days sanding and filling the lumps and bumps.

That was the primer. Painting the top coat was Act Two of the drama. The script was the same as Act One. The action was identical. The only thing that changed was the color of the paint.

"Don't worry, mon, this how we always do it in Chaggy."

Approximately three months later, the topcoat failed. The top coat had zero adherence to the primer. I literally pulled the boot stripe off in one continuous strip. I rolled it up neatly, placed it on the desk of the boatyard manager and asked him for his response.

"Garth's been having a bit of bad luck lately" he said.

Garth's luck at that moment was not at issue. I was given a full refund for all products that I had purchased in the boatyard's paint store and a free month on the dry. The yard manager's last words as he put his hand on my shoulder while I was leaving the office were "Garth is NOT going to work in this yard ever again." The perception of eternity in Trinidad is flexible. Garth was in the boatyard the next day painting a boat.

An undervalued member in the 'five others' was an ultra-light orbiting particle named Tad. After I fired Garth for the fifth and last time, I hired Tad away for the next season. We paid him the normal rate of $100 TT plus another $10 TT a day as a bonus. Seventeen dollars was a good and fair wage in the boatyard for a day's work.

You can get to know a lot about a person when you work side by side for months. As Tad and I shared company, our conversations grew candid. Tad had no formal education. His zest for life and a native ability for observation filled this void. The diversity between our backgrounds was the fuel that maintained our afternoon discussions. While always retaining our objectivity, we had the good fortune and opportunity to discuss the issues of race and inequality without excessive emotion. It was a pleasure to wrestle with these charged topics and, in the end, always find agreement.

Tad and I would normally have a beer or two in the cockpit after our work was done. It was on one of those days that I asked him where he lived. I knew that he lived in the Carenage, a small village on the outskirts of Chaguaramas. I really wanted to know how he lived. With great pride and clarity of thought, Tad described to me how he had left home at the age of thirteen. He lived hand to mouth for years until he found a job sanding boats in Chaguaramas. With a few bucks in his pocket, he purchased a small load of excess concrete blocks from a local construction site. He carried each block one by one up into the hills where the land was unincorporated and thereby subject to the encroachment of squatters. He crudely graded an area fifty feet by fifty feet. He dry stacked the blocks. Then he went down the hill for a load of corrugated metal and formed and tied down a rudimentary roof.

Within several weeks he had built what he described as a house, a dry safe abode that belonged to him alone. Doggedly he carried all descriptions of domestic necessities up the hill: furniture, rain barrel, bed, and wash basin. Every found object discarded by another was a treasure to Tad. After the obligatory one year waiting period, his half brother helped him register his Squat in the courts of Port of Spain. He was then fully vested in his place in the sun. Despite what seemed overwhelming evidence to the contrary, Tad's shanty - in a sea of shanties - belonged to a tight community. It is unlikely that electric power and water service will ever be available to him. The police avoid the vicinity. It was ignored and forgotten. Naturally the residents dreamed of moving down the hill to houses with real walls.

But in the end what possible sense could I make of Tad's ebullient arrival each morning? He was happy. He was proud, and he never made it seem out of place that I too was proud and happy for him. Using scientific and calibrated methods that would have given Garth nightmares, Wendy, Tad and I successfully refinished all the fiberglass surfaces on Quest, both paint and gelcoat. But that would be next season. And a very busy one it would be.

Five

Chacachacare: The Leper Colony

For Quest's crew of two, our seasons in Trinidad ended and began in Chacachacare. Our extended residence in the boatyard made us itch to get back on the water. We knew that all too soon we would be back in Chaguaramas finishing the job that we had started. While I was backing out of the travel slip, a pirogue - begrudging my right of way - came within a foot of Quest's stern at high speed, shipping an inch of water into my cockpit. When the travel lift lowered us into the water I wasn't really sure how long it would take us to come up with a sailing plan. Some plans come faster than others. It took about thirty five seconds in this case.

I looked at Wendy and said "Let's get out of here. Bring up the charts for Chacachacare."

The island of Chacachacare lies halfway between Trinidad and Venezuela. It's best known as a former leper colony. If the lighthouse is accidently functioning that month, then the population of the island is one. What comes to the mind of a Trini when you mention Chacachacare?

"Going down island, mon?" After this

straightforward navigational query, he will lean in and with a strained look on his face, he will say "It's a leper colony! Why you want to go there mon? It's haunted and you'll get sick!"

Chacachacare is six miles from the mainland of one of the most populated islands in the Caribbean and it is completely deserted. After enduring the sardine packed life style of boatyard dwellers, we welcomed the company of a few undemanding ghosts. We sailed over and dropped the hook in what was described in the cruising guide as an all weather anchorage. The surf sent heavy spray over the bow. That cruising guide was evidently written from the bridge of a battleship.

I looked over to the adjacent shore about a quarter of a mile away where a very tiny bay was sheltered by a headland. It was dead calm. We sounded our way over. When we got into the calm behind the headland, there was still 120 feet of water under Quest. I inched Quest to the shore and finally found the shelf about 50 feet from shore. I pulled out and swung Quest around and dropped 200 feet of anchor chain in 80 feet of water. I backed into the shore and came close enough to throw a line on the beach. I jumped overboard, walked to shore, and secured the line to a palm while Wendy tightened the stern line on a sheet winch.

With the bow hanging over an underwater ledge, the stern was in two feet of water and the headland that sheltered us from the sea was thirty feet to starboard. We were in the tightest of all anchorages. It seemed filled to capacity with one Bayfield 36. This seldom used and practically unknown anchorage on Chacachacare was one of the best we found in the Caribbean. At least it suited us for the next two months. You could weather out a storm and never spill your drink.

An abandoned former convent occupied the top of the small rocky headland that sheltered Quest from the sea. Many years ago, the nuns that occupied the convent were the caretakers of the lepers that lived with the resident doctor in the leprosarium on the opposite shore. The official Trinidad handout for Chacachacare describes the abandoned hospital and the quarters of the leprosarium as being consumed by the jungle.

This description seemed at odds with what the infrequent visiting cruiser had told us. For years, cruisers have described the condition of the hospital as frozen in time. The day after we dropped the hook in Chacachacare, we dinghied to the beach in front of the hospital. The jungle was indeed encroaching on the buildings. It was easy to make light of the vivid descriptions of Chacachacare from the safety of the mainland six miles to the east. Approaching this eerie bit of history for real had a palpable eerie feeling. There was a small part of me that wanted to get back in the dinghy and leave. But if I left now, I knew that I would just have to come back later.

We climbed the steps to the hospital.

"Did you see that?! It looked like some sort of human" I whispered to Wendy. "Behind the tree… right over there."

"Just stop it!" she said.

The stories regarding the state of the leprosarium

were all too strangely accurate. Although nature and weather had taken its toll on the hospital over the past 40 odd years, vials of medication were still sitting on counters. A ledger lay open in front of a window. A pencil lay in the fold of the binding. This was probably the day book for recording the medication administered to patients. There were more vials in well stocked cupboards.

We explored deeper into the hospital. Dirty dishes rested in a rusty sink. The metal bed frames and springs were neatly lined up in the ward. The x-ray machine sat poised over the x-ray table. Developed x-ray films were stacked in folders. Nothing was out of place. There was even a Doctor's lab coat hanging in a closet. A partially written letter lay on a desk. There was a projector in the recreation room with a reel of film ready to go in the machine. It was as if someone spent considerable time arranging each article for our visit. It was practically inconceivable that over the years not one person had ransacked the place. It takes a powerfully eerie place to put vandals off their stride for forty years.

Chacachacare is a horseshoe-shaped island about four miles from tip to tip. Except for the leprosarium and the convent, the island was almost untouched by the hand of man. The abandoned convent that overlooked our anchorage was weather beaten but structurally sound. It was a heavy stone and mortar building. Unlike the hospital, it had been the victim of minor vandalism. However, it didn't take much imagination to picture the day to day life of the nuns, praying in the chapel, dining at the long single table in the kitchen, administering to the lepers across the bay. What was difficult to imagine were the effects of the intrusion of World War Two on their routine. A military presence was established directly adjacent to the nunnery. For several years during the war, there were 600 US Marines on the island living in close proximity to the leprosarium and convent. Nuns, Marines, lepers and convicted prisoner volunteers, each with their own distinct hierarchy, culture and code of conduct, lived side by side.

We hiked almost daily on the military roads that the Americans had built during World War Two. Most of the network of roads had been worn down to paths by the consuming jungle. Our favorite hike was to climb a high promontory that gave us a vista of both Trinidad and Venezuela. It is said that Chacachacare is where the Caribbean and South America join hands. It could also be noted that this international frontier was the place where many hands met in the lucrative exchange of contraband. Sitting on that rocky promontory, it became obvious that we were right in the middle of smugglers alley. Day and night, pirogues transited between the two countries with the usual level of intervention.

Trinidad winter weather is mild. An exception was the storm that blew in on the third week of our 'squat' in Chacachacare. A sustained wind of 35 mph blew straight from the east and kicked up fifteen foot seas. We were snug in our anchorage. The storm did accomplish what the Trinidad government continually struggles with. The storm terminated the commerce in smugglers alley. At the height of the storm, a pirogue came into the harbor and beached on the opposite shore. Apparently they were using the same boating guide as Wendy and I. Within ten minutes, they re-launched and motored over to our sanctuary and beached behind Quest.

"Hello, Hello."

"I think they're calling you, Wendy."

"You better take this call" she said.

I threw out our full supply of fenders and called them alongside.

"What are you boys doing out in a storm like this?" I asked.

"We fishin'."

"You're fission?" I asked.

"Si, we fishermen from Fernando."

San Fernando is a city on the southwest coast of Trinidad with a good sized fishing village. I thought his Spanish accent a bit out of character for San Fernando.

"Are you Spanish?" I asked.

He pointed in the general direction of Venezuela. "Me from Venezuela."

"I thought you were from San Fernando."

"I from Venezuela… he from Trinidad." Gesturing he pointed to one of his fellow inter-island traders.

"Are you coming or going?" I asked.

While they looked at each other with blank puzzled expressions, I took a surreptitious look in the bottom of the pirogue. No tackle. No nets. No fish. Except for the seven 5-gallon jerry cans of gasoline, it was completely empty. That should be plenty of fuel for a day of fishing. Sensing the conversation flag, I said goodbye and turned to go below.

"You have snacks?"

"What?"

"Chips?"

"No, we don't have any snacks."

"We don't eat three days."

I gave him a most sympathetic look and asked "three days?"

"Very long time mon" he said.

Perhaps some hospitality was in order. I was cooking lunch at the time, so I gave them a big bowl of curried chick peas and rice. They accepted the food most graciously. Five minutes later...tap, tap, tap on the hull.

"Yes?" I said.

"You have paper paws?"

"WHAT?"

"Paper paws?"

What was he trying to say? He was gesturing by shaking his hand upside down on his channa. Ah, pepper sauce! I went to the galley and retrieved a half pint bottle of Tabasco.

"Taunks mon."

We were in a tricky situation. We were in a very remote location. We were well outside the reach of Trinidad law. On the other hand, we were well within the reach of the five smugglers brand of justice. Our choice was simple. We could run for the cover of the mainland like scared dogs or we could stand our ground. The idea of running was dismissed entirely. Our anchor chain was too encrusted with barnacles to make a quick getaway. We prepared to stand our ground. Would we live to regret this decision when the boys started passing the rum around? Tap, tap, tap...

"You got rum?"

"NO, no rum, sorry." I gave them five cans of apple juice.

"Taunks, mon."

The fact that they didn't have any rum added a very positive wrinkle to the dynamic. At least they wouldn't be getting drunk and disorderly. He left looking forlorn and returned to the shore where he sat with his mates staring at Quest and occasionally gesturing in our direction.

I slept in the cockpit that night armed with a baseball bat. At first light I awoke to an unshaven face staring down at me over the gunwales.

"You got food?"

We were now a full-fledged floating smugglers roadhouse. I made them tea and toast.

"I wonder what's up with these guys" I said to Wendy.

We decided to test their resolve. We climbed the hill behind the convent and hid in a thicket. It wasn't five minutes that we were out of sight when they got into their pirogue and paddled over to Quest. Did they pick us clean? Not quite. Watching their interaction with Quest with binoculars, it looked like the ring leader was the only one that had the right to touch Quest. They circled all around Quest. The leader held a sheet block in his hand. He described it to his mates. He did the same with a boat hook. Then they went to the bow and he pulled our anchor chain. He demonstrated how well we had set the heavy chain.

Chacachacare: The Leper Colony

They pulled themselves around to the starboard side. The leader rolled a winch drum a few times. Not once did he attempt to board Quest or take away any plunder. After half an hour they went back to shore and settled in for their morning nap.

Following their afternoon nap, they approached Quest and put in their order for channa and rice. Channa is the local vernacular for curried chick peas. Five orders of channa were served up on deck.

"Clean the dishes" I told him.

He nodded. We were now a floating roti roadhouse. That night, Wendy and I both slept armed in the cockpit. Just like clockwork, the hairy face appeared over the gunwales at dawn.

"We go now" he said."

That was a polite gesture. Wendy looked at me and asked what he said.

I said "They're leaving. They've had enough channa."

The surprise visit from the smugglers was certainly entertaining. It was even educational. Shortly after their departure, we took up our daily habit of hiking to the promontory overlooking Trinidad and Venezuela. Sitting on the craggy summit, we could put a face on the smugglers hundreds of feet below us.

For a small country, Trinidad has a well equipped Coast Guard. It can easily deal with the comparatively small number of marine incidents that occur in Trinidad waters. It is said that the Trinidad Coast Guard is prepared to contend with any problem at any time. Generally, locating the problem is always their first obstacle.

Three days after the smugglers left Questworld Roti Road House, Wendy and I were sitting in the cockpit when a Coast Guard vessel paid a visit to Chacachacare. This wasn't an ordinary boat. It was a fully loaded, brand new 40 foot modified V-hull with three 250 HP engines. They bore down on us. They slowed. When they attempted to pass behind our stern, I stood up in my cockpit, pointed at the stern line and yelled STOP!! The gesture was apparently mistaken as hostile. The four well-dressed young Coast Guard officers fell to the bottom of the cockpit and pulled their side arms.

After a moment to compose himself, the commanding officer stood up and yelled back "What!...What?"

"If you go ten more feet, you're going to foul those shiny chrome propellers on my stern line."

When the four lads realized that they weren't about to be gunned down, they all stood up and belly laughed. We tied them along side, making sure not to bruise their paint job. We extended our hospitality and invited them on board for beverages and snacks. I recall very little time being spent on immigration formalities.

"Would you like to see our papers?" I asked.

"No, no mon, every ting cool."

I brewed up a fresh pot of coffee, a good Colombian blend.

"Havin' any trouble?" the captain asked.

"No" I said. "Just the usual lineup of smugglers."

Chacachacare: The Leper Colony

They took this as a grand joke. Then it was my turn to ask questions.

"Trinidad, Venezuela, South America, the Islands… Is there much smuggling here? "

"It isn't a problem" he said with pride. "We cleaned out the smugglers years ago."

"I bet they're afraid of your boat" I said.

"Yeah mon" he laughed. "We catch anybody with dis boat!"

We spent a pleasant time chatting with the Trinidad Coast Guard. A friendlier Coast Guard I have never met.

Our stay in Chacachacare drew to a quiet conclusion. It seemed like just yesterday that we were setting the hook and tying the stern line. The next day I chiseled the barnacles off the chain and left the former leper colony known as Chacachacare. We were on our way back to Chaguaramas. God help the contractors when we got back.

View many photographs of Chacachacare at
www.questandcrew.com

Six

Ten Degrees from the Equator

How hard can it be to polish a hull with 1000 grit sandpaper? Sanding a hull is not a technical operation. It should be easy, especially with 1000 grit wet sandpaper and a block. After our extended stay in Chacachacare, we found on our return to Chaguaramas that the fraternity of contractors had voted us 'persona non grata'. The contractors all agreed that we were too much trouble. Our standards were too high. Owing to our notoriety, we found difficulty acquiring day laborers. Tad was sent forth on a mission to bring back manual labor. Two hours later, Tad returned with Steve and Ian. All three, thoroughly lubricated on overproof rum, stood in front of me weaving and lurching. I took Tad aside.

"Is this the best you can find?"

"Dis it mon."

That was that. Steve and Ian would sand the hull.

"You're hired" I said. "Be here at 8:00 tomorrow."

We were standing beside Quest the next morning when Ian, Steve, and Tad got off the bus and entered the boatyard.

"They can't really mess this up, can they?" Wendy asked.

"Keep the booze locked up" I said.

We left Steve and Ian with a box of 1000 grit wet sandpaper and very specific instructions: they were to take the day and polish Quest's hull. I left Tad in charge. I walked to the paint shop to talk to Kirk and get some wax to buff the hull after the wet polishing.

"Hi Kirk" I said when I opened the door. "That's a great paint job on that 40 footer outside."

He was distracted. After a moment he looked up.

"No… no, that's not a paint job. That's a gelcoat job."

My knowledge of gelcoat was about to take a leap forward.

"Isn't gelcoat just sprayed into a mold before the layup?" I asked.

He looked away and continued to stack the shelves. After a moment he looked back at me.

"Gelcoat is sprayed in boat molds but it can also be sprayed on the outside of a hull" he said. "We keep 100 gallon drums in stock. At least fifty boats a year get gelcoated around here. We get plenty business."

He jumped over the counter, put his hand on my shoulder, and steered me to the door.

"Come mon, I'll show you" he said.

We crossed the driveway in front of the paint shop.

"This is a good gelcoat job" he said.

It was absolutely fantastic. It was as flawless as a boat fresh out of the mold and polished. He showed me another boat about 200 feet away that was being sanded down. The third boat had been sprayed the previous day. It was a mess. You wouldn't want a finish like that on an oil drum. It was covered in dirt and dust and loaded with craters.

"This one must have gone bad?" I asked.

"They all look like that when they fresh sprayed" he said. He pointed to the first job he had shown me. "That one looked a lot worse when it was sprayed!"

"I had no idea. I've passed these boats a hundred times and I thought that they were all painted" I said.

"Well, now go gelcoat your boat" he suggested with friendly humor.

I walked back to Quest in a cloud. I was thoroughly enjoying my new found wealth of information. I was almost back to Quest before I realized that I had forgotten the buffing supplies.

When I returned, Tad looked comfortable reading a newspaper underneath the boat. Steve and Ian were on the scaffolding at the stern intently concentrating on a small area at the top right.

"What's going on?" I asked.

"Big problem mon. But we got it fixed. Da scratches… right here on da hull. We fill and sand um. Scratches gone now" Ian reported proudly.

"Not the boat number!" I yelled.

I jumped on the scaffolding. They both backed away slowly.

"No mon, it just scratches mon."

Ian's self confidence was waning. They had

managed in twenty minutes to completely remove all traces of Quest's serial number. If we happened to be caught anywhere in the Caribbean without a registration number our boat could be seized by Customs.

I gave them each $100 TT, shook their hands, and said "Thanks for coming by. You're done."

Tad retired to the opposite side of Quest.

"Tad, get over here!" I yelled.

Like a scared pup he came to the stern expecting retribution. I jumped off the scaffolding and motioned for Wendy and Tad to come over to the fence where I was standing.

I looked Tad in the eyes and said "Can you spray gelcoat?"

"I spray gelcoat, but I can't mix" he said.

"Perfect, do you think you could spray gelcoat on Quest if we all sanded it down and I mixed the gelcoat?"

"Yeah mon, easy."

"Are you OK with this Wendy?"

She came on board the project with understandable reluctance. With blind enthusiasm, Wendy, Tad and I had agreed to re-gelcoat Quest. The team consisted of one person who didn't have the slightest idea what gelcoat was. The second had discovered the wonders of polyester resin twenty minutes earlier. The third may or may not have a working knowledge of the gelcoating process. More importantly there wasn't anybody around to tell us we couldn't gelcoat Quest.

In the most basic terms, re-gelcoating a boat consists of sanding the entire hull with 120 grit sand paper, tinting the gelcoat, mixing the resin with catalyst, taping, spraying the gelcoat, allowing the gelcoat to harden, wet sanding the gelcoat, then finally polishing with wax. This is the short way of describing four months of back breaking work, 10° from the equator. We developed our strategy. We would find a gelcoat contractor and ask him as many questions as we could before his patience wore thin. Then we would immediately follow up with confirmation from Kirk in the paint shop. As we made our inquiries the pieces of the puzzle came together. There were only three questionable areas in our basic training. How do we tint the pure white polyester resin to match Quest's original color, how much Methyl ethyl ketone peroxide (MEKP) to add as a hardener, and how to re-apply the sanded off registration number to Quest's stern. Answer those three questions and we would have a gelcoat job.

We first tackled the question of how to tint the gelcoat. The paint shop sold the tinting agents and a guide to blending gelcoat colors. With blue, yellow and brown tints, a guide, and a handful of 30 cc syringes, we experimented with a quart of gelcoat. We slowly increased the pigments, recording every tweak in a journal. After three tries, the match was perfect. This custom formula would be scaled up to the ten gallons needed to cover the topsides and deck.

If there is magic to gelcoating, it's in the MEKP, specifically the amount of MEKP to mix with the polyester resin so that it hardens properly. Too much and it hardens in the paint gun before you even spray. Too little and the gel coat will never harden. The container had the instructions we needed printed right on the label, 1% - 2 %. After trial and error, we arrived at the exact amount of 18 milliliters of MEKP in 1000 milliliters of resin.

The method of re-creating, or more precisely, forging Quest's registration number came to me in a flash. When we purchased Quest, I had taken a very tight close-up of the registration number. I studied the photo for two days. There was something very familiar about the size and font. I woke up at 2:30 one morning. 'Bingo! It's the reverse image of an old dymo-tape!' I had a long seven hours to wait before the stationery stores opened in Port of Spain. We gave Tad the day off and Wendy and I went in search of a Dymo embosser/labeler.

"Do you have a Dymo-labeler?" I asked the clerk behind the counter of a large stationary store.

She was about twenty five years old and I am sure that she had never seen an old Dymo. I might as well have been speaking another language. She did show me her full selection of labelers while I was backing out the door. This was hopeless. We had been to three stationary stores all over the city and had struck out.

Walking back to the bus terminal, we passed Gupta's Print Shop down a flight of stairs.

"Do you have a dymo?" I asked the old merchant. I was now quite comfortable asking such a ridiculous question.

"They still make those? I got one of those when I was 18 years old" he said.

Another dead end, I thought to myself. Now let's spend a half hour listening to Gupta's stories.

"I've still got that machine" he said.

He now had my full attention.

"You have the dymo…you have the dymo in the store… here?" I asked.

"Yes, yes" he said.

With conservation of movement, he shuffled into the back room and retrieved a cardboard box.

"Here it is" he said.

My hands were shaking as I took the heirloom. It was solid chrome. No wonder they don't make these any more.

"Let's give it a try" I said.

"No. No, I can't sell this" he said.

"I just want you to run off a couple of numbers" I pleaded as I placed a piece of paper with the registration number on the counter.

"You do it, I don't have my glasses" he said.

I ran off one copy and three spares before the tape ran out.

"That will be 2 $TT" he said.

Off we went enjoying our good fortune.

The following day I epoxied the raised side of the dymo-tape onto a piece of teak. When the epoxy was hard, I coated the reverse side with wax release. Tad and I mixed a batch of gelcoat and sprayed it onto an old piece of fiberglass that we found lying beside Quest. Waiting ten minutes for the resin to thicken, I pressed the waxed side of the dymo-tape in to the gelcoat and peeled it back. The test worked. We had a perfect forgery of Quest's registration number. We simply had to duplicate the procedure on the stern.

We could now begin the dusty job of roughing the hull with 120 grit dry sandpaper. Two boxes of sandpaper and two weeks later we were ready for the spray. Kirk graciously delivered the 2 five gallon pails of gelcoat to Quest.

"When I said you should gelcoat your boat I was just joking" he said with a grin.

He looked over the job and gave us his blessing. The next big item on the checklist was the tricky job of tinting. The tools for the job are as basic as you can get, a drill, a mixing paddle, tints and syringes for measuring. Tad took his station standing directly above the open pail with the mixing paddle chucked in the drill. I double checked the tint formula and loaded the syringes.

"Let's go Tad."

He started the drill and the gelcoat began to whirlpool. I injected half the amount of each color into the bucket. It looked really good. I shot the rest into the pail. The color was almost right on. I added a small touch of brown tint and moved onto the second pail and mixed up the identical color. When the two pails were tinted, I poured half the contents of each pail in an empty five gallon pail, and then we mixed the two remaining halves together in the first pail. This ensured that the entire ten gallons were exactly the same. The smelly, finicky job of tinting the resin was over without a hitch.

Once you start spraying gelcoat you must finish the job. For a proper bond, each layer is best applied to a previous layer that hasn't quite cured. It was going to be a long day with five layers of gel coat sprayed one quart at a time. At 6:00 the next morning we began taping and tarping Quest and any surface within fifty feet of Quest that needed to be protected from overspray. This included tarping the neighboring boats that surrounded us. The mixing bench was organized with the spray gun, pail of resin, MEKP, thinner, nylon gloves and acetone all at the ready.

Tad and I practiced a number of dry runs until we were comfortable. I went through the motions of measuring and mixing a liter spray pot of resin with MEKP catalyst. I then tossed the empty spray pot to Tad who connected it to the airline. He practiced disconnecting the air hose and throwing the pot down to me. Wendy was in charge of ensuring that Tad had an untangled and unimpeded air hose. We were a practiced team. At exactly 8 AM I pitched the first quart of resin to Tad. Quart by quart we emptied the five gallon pail. At 1 PM I had poured my last quart. The tape, plastic, and tarps were removed. We were done and done in.

We took the weekend off. Monday kicked off the sanding of the decks. Unlike the topsides it took a bit longer than we had expected but we finally completed the sanding. The next job was spraying the resin on the decks. This added a small technical wrinkle. The MEKP had to be increased. The resin had to cure faster so that Tad and Wendy could walk on the freshly sprayed coat as they made passes from stern to bow. Another five gallons of resin, another six hours of mixing and spraying and Quest was fully gelcoated and waiting to be sanded.

There isn't anything extraordinary about finishing a gelcoat job, just a lot of hard work sanding off the imperfections. Sometimes it seemed like we would never see the end to the boxes of wet sandpaper and the thousands of gallons of water. Sanding consumed months of our time, beginning with 220 grit wet paper, then 400, and working all the way through 1000 grit, finishing with a buffing of 2000 grit paste and finally waxing the gelcoat three times. Quest was absolutely beautiful. She sparkled. After about two months when the gelcoat still hadn't fallen off, the obligatory compliments began to flood in.

"Hey, you going to sell her?"

"Why don't you come over and do our boat next?"

The cruisers' wit was as consistent as the Trinidad weather.

Life was returning back to routine. The paint and the gelcoat were beautiful. We built up 10 coats of varnish on the teak. We re-chromed and re-installed the winches. The computer balanced prop was bolted onto the shaft. The only thing left was to put on a clean shirt and present ourselves to Immigration for our six month interview and request another six month extension on our visas. We had plans to go back to our squat in Chacachacare after we splashed Quest. When we arrived at Immigration all the old smiling faces from previous interviews were gone. The new regime seemed a humorless bunch.

"Good morning Officer" I said courteously, hoping to get the interview off to a good start.

The officer in charge looked at me and pointedly asked me why I had stayed in Trinidad so long.

"I'm working on my boat" I said.

"I don't give a damn about your boat" he snarled.

He grabbed our passports and stamped them so hard that two pens rolled to the edge of the desk and fell to the floor. He then wrote across the stamps 'Three months final'.

He picked up the passport and held it three inches from my face and said "Can you read this?"

"Can you move it back about a foot? I'm nearsighted" I replied.

He threw the passport on the desk and bellowed "Next." That day he managed to expel a total of ten cruisers from Trinidad.

Despite the officer's corrosive personality he was right. We had outstayed our visit to Trinidad. Our days had become regimented. At ten degrees from the equator, you don't need a newspaper to tell you that the sun will rise at 6 AM. At 7 AM the morning wind freshens and the flocks of green parrots fly and squawk their way from the jungle over to a nearby off shore island for the day. They return at exactly 5 PM. The temperature didn't vary by more than five degrees day or night. For two months in the winter it rained at exactly 12:30 every day. The closer you get to the equator the more obvious is the Earth's precision clockworks. When Wendy and I first came to Trinidad, this regularity was a fascinating novelty. By the end of our stay I was becoming nostalgic for variety. I missed the seasons, the leaves falling in the autumn, the new shoots in the spring. It was time to point the bow north. It was time for change.

A month after Immigration had given us our walking papers we were ready to leave Trinidad. Quest was well stocked with food and beer. The tanks were all filled to capacity. The only thing remaining was to get our exit stamp from Immigration. The crazed Immigration officer will probably give me hell for leaving Trinidad too soon. When I opened the door to the office I was stunned. All the friendly faces were back behind the counter.

"Where's Grumpy?" I asked with a grin.

"Grumpy doesn't live here any more, he made too many important enemies" the officer replied.

He stamped my passport and said "I hope that you enjoyed your stay in Trinidad."

Seven

Road Trip

There were a lot of surprises on the morning of January 1, 2000. I strolled out to the end of my driveway in Charlotte, North Carolina to see if civilization had come to an end. Bob, my friend, neighbor, and certified Y2K aficionado approached. I'm not going to bring up Y2K unless he does, I thought to myself. Our brief season's greetings gave me no entry to the topic. After a year obsessed with Y2K he was mute on the subject.

I looked at Quest in the side yard as I crushed the pine needles into the driveway on the way back to the house. Before the year was up, we and our cruising sailboat Quest would be moving south, probably to Florida. Where do we go? How do we get there? We would have to sell the house and just about everything we owned. We were going to be full-time cruisers so we could only take what we could stow on board. I went back in the house. I put the plans aside for the moment and stoked up a nice blaze in the fireplace. The door bell rang. It's probably Bob wanting to sell me an '86 Ford 250 with a couple of rocket launchers thrown in I laughed to myself. I opened the door for two strangers, a well dressed couple in their late thirties.

Road Trip

"We'd like to know if you would consider selling us your house" the well spoken man asked.

Now that is a good opening line.

"Come on in" I said. "I've got a great fire going."

I called Wendy down to join us in the living room.

"These folks want to buy our house" I said.

We sat down with Jean and Greg and fleshed out the sale of our house on the back of a piece of junk mail. We shook on it. We shared some wine. We had a deal.

Before the day was up we would learn two interesting details about Jean and Greg from our neighbor Junior. It turned out that Greg bought, sold and rented property all over the city. He was well versed at knocking on strangers' doors and asking to buy their houses. The more germane detail was that he was good friends with Junior. Junior had mentioned to Greg in passing that we were about to put our house on the market. Why Greg didn't mention this when we were putting the deal together remained a mystery until I spoke to Junior that day.

"Junior, we have a buyer for our house."

"That's right" Junior said. "I knew there was something that I was supposed to tell you."

"It was a good New Year's Day surprise" I said. "Do you want something for helping with the deal?"

"Naw" he said. "Just getting you out of the neighborhood is all the reward I need."

The chain of events that was set in motion with purchasing Quest was carrying us along. We were on our way. No doubt except for the reluctance of Ted, our split bed boat hauler. We had approximately five months before we would have to be out of our house in Charlotte. Five months to move to some where, anywhere. Five months to find a way to ransom Quest from our side yard.

The decision to move to Fernandina Beach, Florida came almost instantly. Fernandina had everything that we wanted and very little of what we didn't. We had stopped in the town a number of times on trips to Florida when we were purchasing Quest. It is a small town on a barrier island in North Florida, right on the Georgia border. The winters and summers are mild and the pace of life is about one cup of coffee shy of comatose. Its location on the Intracoastal Waterway, the ICW, as well as the ocean would give us plenty of opportunity to learn to sail. It was rich in history and boating traditions. It was practically free of hurricanes. We would need a small apartment for the time that Quest was on the hard and then dockage when the big day arrived when we would splash Quest. Just one year and we would be on our way to the Caribbean.

Lining up a slip and an apartment in an unknown city would require a road trip. A pleasant six hour drive from Charlotte and we were approaching the bridge on the ICW that linked Fernandina with the mainland. All the road fatigue vanished when we drove onto the bridge. When we got to the top of the 70 foot span the panorama was magnificent. The sun glinted off the ICW that wound for miles through tidal marshes on both sides of the bridge. It was like I was seeing water for the first time. In my mind Quest was being transformed from a paper weight in my side yard to a boat capable of crossing oceans. I had every confidence in Quest's capabilities.

Road Trip

The following day, the realtor was at the front door of the hotel before I got off the phone with her. It's a small town. This was our first meeting with the realtor and she was out to impress. Before both of the SUV's doors were closed she took in the breath of a free diver and commenced her pitch. She talked for the next fifteen minutes without exhaling. Before we had gotten half way across the island she had covered the last twenty years of her life in painstaking detail. Her well thought out curriculum vitae commenced in her late teens as a cheer leader for the local high school, 'The Pirates.' It ended with a few anecdotal comments about the future of Fernandina. She talked so long without taking a breath that I started to hyperventilate.

"I'm just talking way too much" she said gasping for air and taking a sip of her double espresso. "So… what brings you two folks to Fernandina?"

"We need an apartment and a slip for a forty foot boat" I responded.

"I just love boats…I love being on the water…it's so beautiful on the water…it's so relaxing…you said you needed a slip…you mean you want to dock a boat… have you bought it yet …what kind of boats do you like...you know that there aren't any slips available in Fernandina."

"Wait a minute! You're telling me that there aren't any slips in Fernandina?"

"I didn't say that exactly" she said. "I said that there aren't any available…There are three marinas on the island, the yacht club, the city marina and they are booked up until someone dies or a boat sinks, then they take the first boat on a four page waiting list."

"If we can't find a slip then we can't move to Fernandina" I said. "Didn't you say there were three marinas in town?"

"Well ah… yes, there are three marinas." After a pause she said "There is another marina, of sorts… down in the marsh. It doesn't have a lot of slips. It's kind of off the beaten path. It's more like a boatyard… sort of."

With a bit of persuasion she drove us to Tiger Point Marina. It was definitely a boatyard. The only amenity was a rusting coke machine on cinder blocks leaning against the paint building.

"Who owns this place?" I asked.

"Well that's the other problem."

Her elaboration was cut in mid sentence when a surly looking middle aged gent came around the corner. He looked really down on his luck. His coveralls looked like a bum's rejects. His stringy yellow gray hair stuck out in shocks from under a greasy ball cap. When he came closer the realtor started backing up, strategically closing the gap between herself and her car door.

"Do you run the marina?" I asked, not aware that I lacked the proper respectful tone.

"No" he said brusquely. "I own the marina. She runs the marina."

He pointed with his thumb to a woman sitting on an overturned five gallon bucket smoking a cigarette.

"I need to put my boat on the hard for six months then I'll need dockage. I don't see any empty slips" I said.

"Fine fine, bring your boat…we'll find you a slip

when you need one" he said.

He did a quick about face and veered off seeming to walk in two directions at the same time.

I got back into the realtor's car thinking that he was definitely a bit odd.

"Look…" she said. "The first thing that you should know about Captain K is that he is one of the richest men in a rich town…. and the second… he's less than half as cuddly as he looks!"

"Fine" I said. "Let's go find an apartment on the beach."

Empty rental apartments in Fernandina during the winter keep the bulletin boards in the realtors' offices well papered. The same apartment that you have to beg for in June is a steal in February. We hit the perfect apartment on the second try. It wasn't the choicest real estate on the island but it was two blocks from the ocean in the middle of a five mile strand of pristine beach.

I would venture to say that I wasn't completely ready for the next mis-step that was in store for Quest. For the last year I had plenty of time to contemplate the fragile hand shake agreement that I had with Ted the boat hauler. I didn't make much of his prophetic ramblings when he finished backing Quest onto the property.

"You know" he said "I think that I have the only split bed hauler on the east coast that could have gotten your boat on this property."

"Run that by me again" I said while I was writing him a check.

With discernible pride he described his truck. "I

bought the standard split bed rig and had the manufacturer install special hydraulic lifts on the bed so that I could raise it up a bit higher than normal. I have a bump in my boatyard that my other low boy was bottoming on. Do you see that rise in your drive way? A normal low boy rig would bottom out right there. With ten tons of cargo it could get stuck…really stuck."

For a split second I was feeling pretty lucky. Boy was I fortunate to have found the only hauler on the east coast that could deliver Quest to my side yard.

"You will come back and haul her out of here, right?"

"Sure, just give me a call" he said.

By the time he had pulled onto the road I was starting to get that uneasy feeling. I stewed and thought about what he had said for the rest of the morning. He can't possibly have the only truck with custom hydraulics. Fifty percent curiosity and fifty percent panic caused me to call up the truck manufacturer.

"Yes sir, we built Ted's truck and yes we added custom hydraulics."

"Are there any more like Ted's around?"

"Well there is one in Washington State" he said.

I slowly put the phone down. This is one of those pieces of information that I shouldn't have gone looking for. Ted will be back. There is nothing to worry about. The conscious mind could easily deflect this minor anxiety. On the other hand it was the perfect fuel to stoke the imagination when I'd wake at 2:30 in the morning thinking about it.

Road Trip

By the beginning of the summer the house was practically empty. Our temporary lease with Greg was up in a month. We had sold everything that we had accumulated over the last fifteen years. Our only remaining possessions were a few pieces of furniture. We hadn't kept much, but it would fill our small apartment in Fernandina.

It was May, time to call Ted. I rang him up, I left a message. Two days later I called him again, I left another message. The next Monday I left him an urgent message to get in touch with me. He called back.

"I'm having the truck serviced" he said.

"You're going to move my boat?" I asked.

"I don't know" he said.

I got off the phone with Ted and started calling all the big boat haulers on the East Coast. No one would touch this. It was their big season and they didn't want to mess around in someone's side yard in North Carolina.

This calls for a well designed bluff. I drove down to Ted's boatyard and located Ted.

"When are you moving my boat?" I asked.

"I'm not moving your boat."

"We had a deal Ted."

"So you say."

"Ted, I've looked into this problem and I think that if you refuse to move Quest then we are going to need someone with a lot more legal acumen than both of us to make a decision on this."

He stared at me with a fixed expression. Neither one of us moved. This better work or I'm dead.

"Why don't you just ask me why I won't move your boat."

I raised my palms and asked why.

"When I came up from Florida I underestimated the load a bit. I blew out two rear right tires and ended in the median on the interstate."

"So that's why you were late."

"That's why I was late. I came this close from putting your boat on her side at 60 MPH and wrecking my trailer. I skidded on the shoulder and hit the median at about 15 MPH."

I was scared just thinking about it.

"Think about this solution" I proposed. "You bring Quest out of the woods and up onto the road in front of my house with the split bed, then use a crane to transfer her to your other lowboy.

"That'll work" he said.

When I got home I looked in the phone book for crane companies. There were a lot of choices. I called the company with the full page ad, the one with the shiny new cranes.

"I need to move a boat" I said to the voice on the phone.

"How much does it weigh…what shape is it… where do you want it moved?"

What shape is it? She's filling out a form?

"It's a 20,000 pound boat, it's kind of pointy on one end and I want it picked up about four feet and then put back down" I said. "Pretty simple, right?"

Road Trip

"Do you need any special equipment?" she asked.

"The hauler told me that you would know what equipment I needed!"

"I book cranes, I'm not a crane operator" she snapped. "We can be there next Tuesday morning."

"Fine" I said.

I called Ted and he agreed to the timing. Tuesday came and the crane lumbered up the street right on its own schedule. This was not the shiny crane from the ad in the phone book. This is what was left of a crane. It was a pile of semi-consolidated rust that was leaking a variety of fluids from every conceivable orifice. I was even less inspired when the driver opened his door to reveal two cases of hydraulic fluid stacked beside him in the cab.

"What are we picking up today?" he asked.

No where on the work sheet did it mention a boat. The instructions were right to the point: 'Move 20,000 pound pointy object'.

"We are going to pick up this boat and put it on that trailer waiting over there" I explained. "Have you ever picked up a boat before?" I asked.

"I picked up an oil tank last week. It looked like a boat" he said.

He threw down a set of straps from the cab. Pat, a friend of mine, had come over to help in the maneuver. He had plenty of crane experience maintaining planes in the Air Force. Pat picked up the straps and pointed to a load capacity label.

"This is not going to work!" he said.

The strap read 5000 pounds maximum. Pat took the paper work from the driver.

"Move 20,000 lb pointy object" he read out loud. "Get some 25,000 pound straps down here right now. While you're at it get two 15 foot spreaders" he barked.

Two hours later when the service truck pulled up with the gear, Ted was fuming and threatening. Pat and I dug our heels in and slung Quest. The crane slowly raised Quest off the split bed, groaning and wheezing every inch of the way. The waiting truck pulled under Quest and the transfer was made. It was over in ten minutes. When the operator finished making the transfer he tried to lift his outriggers. The dinosaur then gave an agonizing scream, the hydraulic seal on the right rear outrigger blew and shot a gusher of hydraulic oil across the hardtop.

"No problem" the driver said. "This always happens."

Another call for the service truck, another hour of Ted's grumbling and the mechanics showed. The crane had arrived at 9 AM and it was 3 PM before he could raise the outrigger. The driver handed me a clip board and said "Hey man, you have to sign this." He invoiced me for seven hours at $125 an hour. I took the clip board, crossed out seven hours and replaced it with two hours and made a check out for $250.

"You can't do that" he said.

"Unless you want the Sheriff to cite you for blocking a thoroughfare I suggest that you get this pile of junk out of the road!"

Road Trip

Quest was now on her way to the ocean. Ted had only billed me double what he had charged me to bring Quest up from Fort Lauderdale. Pat and I took a moment to throw a little cat litter on the variety of fluids that had oozed and squirted from the crane. Before we drove off I took one last look at the strange emptiness in the side yard. It was like Quest had disappeared without a trace.

Eight

Echo and the Big Black Whale

Fernandina Beach, Florida is one of the best places to learn to sail. It is probably the best place to learn the complicated maneuvers associated with six foot tides and the accompanying ferocious tidal surge. Quest arrived intact and without incident at Tiger Point Marina. After a year and a half, she was out of the forest of Charlotte, North Carolina and thrust into the company of her peers. The boatyard was full of cruising boats that were left to brave the hurricane season while the winter cruisers went north to grow their gardens. Quest's beautiful clipper bow and graceful lines gave her the undeniable look of a blue water ocean boat. In contrast to Quest's demonstrable seaworthiness was Quest's inexperienced wannabe crew.

To the permanent members and guests of Tiger Point Marina we were an enigma. They could understand our zeal and motivation. It was our methods that were questionable. The tradition regarding the acquisition of a cruising boat has always been a constant. Youthful sailors are introduced to boating as soon as they can walk. When the willing inductee is old enough to see over the gunwales, he or she joins a junior sailing club. Abilities and skills are honed under the watchful eye of parents and mentors. A small sailboat is purchased for junior. Then when his trust fund becomes available a larger boat is purchased. The boat is traded for a larger boat. The cycle is repeated until the maximum burden of boat debt is achieved. With this goal accomplished, the true pleasures of boating are savored. Leisure boating is a culture. Within this culture a common methodology is defined by generations of habitual practice. One doesn't simply buy a full blown cruising sailboat with no experience and expect to sail over the horizon. We were being ridiculous. We were being impractical. Learning to sail is serious business. If we wished to disregard convention then we were far beyond their help.

Compared to the yacht club crowd, the commercial boaters and shrimpers were a breath of fresh air. To this clannish fraternity we were just two more clowns with an expensive shiny boat. But when it came to truly assaying the overall worthiness of any human on land or sea, Captain K was the master.

Captain K was the disheveled and shaggy-haired owner of Tiger Point Marina and Boatyard. When any query of a nautical nature was broached, Captain K forcefully contributed his opinion in his characteristic monosyllabic mumble. Captain K held the exclusive and highly lucrative government contract to pilot large foreign freighters in and out of the sea port of Fernandina Beach. Captain K further complicated his life by hosting and fiercely competing in regional Thistle boat racing. Captain K was a hybrid boater. He was a true seaman and a very competitive dinghy boat racer. In Captain K's position as the local authority on both commercial and leisure boating, we represented an annoying composite of boating clowns as well as hazards to commercial navigation. This was Captain K's playground. Captain K was the very big fish in the very small southern town. He possessed no soft edges that could be taken as weakness of character. Fernandina was the rich feeding ground that supported his voracious financial appetites. Captain K was not a man of the people. He was not approachable.

The day to day operations of the boatyard and marina were placed in the hands of Lalia Browne. Lalia was kind where Captain K would have been opportunistic. She was approachable and open minded. She was the marina's strength. She held the customer in high regard and was loved in return. She was the opposite of Captain K. Lalia was a born naturalist surrounded by nature. She was a keen observer of all the life forms in the marsh. If it flew, slithered or walked on two legs she would learn their habits.

Every boat yard needs a roustabout. Tiger Point was sanctuary to Hank. The only thing about Hank that everyone knew with complete certainty was that Hank was not his real given name. He was just Hank, no last name, no history, just Hank. He possessed no driver license, no Social Security number, no ID of any kind. He lived exclusively in the present. He lived day to day from the kindness of the boat owners and the occasional handout from Captain K. Hank's hair was longer, fuller, yellower and grayer than Captain K's. His hair also stuck out from underneath a greasy ball cap. Hank lived to drive Captain K's lawn tractor around the two acre boatyard with his side kick Tiger in tow behind him on a homemade trailer. Tiger was a mixed breed mutt with gray-yellow hair. His hair was fuller and greasier than both Captain K and Hank's. Tiger found it ridiculous to wear a ball cap.

The culture in which we now found ourselves held serious reservations regarding our successful conversion to full time cruisers. The doubters came well equipped with the knowledge and experience to size up our venture. They were not reluctant to share their opinions with us. They tried in vain but they could not convince us of our folly. We were on a mission. This palatable atmosphere of doubt was instrumental in our decision to buy a small practice sailboat from Captain K while we waited for Quest's dock space. Echo was a 17 foot drop keel sloop that would serve as our introduction into the fraternity of sailors.

Echo had been abandoned at the dock by her owners. The owners, a group of high spirited seniors at the local high school, employed Echo as a floating den of vice. Their most consistent occupation was to get blind drunk and attempt feats of daring. After several years of unsuccessful attempts to sink Echo, they lost interest and left her at the dock. With the dockage fees mounting Captain K placed a lien on Echo and subsequently sold her to us for a small profit.

We were eager to have our first sail with our new sailboat. The tides in North Florida are quite extreme. The six foot flood tide pushes vast quantities of salt water and life forms into the marshes, only to be swept back to sea when the tide reverses. As novices, it seemed prudent to leave when the tide peaked and then stay out until the next flood tide would push us back in. This practical approach seemed sound enough, but as we discovered, the timing left us vulnerable to the vagaries of nature.

We hoped to make a quiet departure from the dock on a Sunday afternoon. I had studied 'the basic learn to sail' guides. I even had a copy of Bowditch wedged between the sofa and the coffee table. It was a great day to give it a try. A beautiful light shimmered on the marshes. The wind was blowing a steady fifteen knots. While we were prepping Echo and collecting our thoughts we heard a commotion in the parking lot above us. I went up to take a look.

"What's going on?" I asked a couple of the men standing against the dock railing."

"This is going to be the biggest race of the year" he said full of excitement.

We better get going before the race starts I thought to myself. They're probably so excited that they won't even notice us leaving. I put up the main and lowered the drop keel. I looked over my shoulder and 45 racers were lined two deep along the dock waiting for us to leave. Just as I cast off the last dock line the shouts and catcalls started on cue.

"Hey…watch that piling!"

"Don't forget to pull your fenders in!"

"You better have your life vests on board; the Coast Guard's waiting for you!"

"Got your whistle?... You're going to need your whistle!"

The hazing continued until we were out of earshot of even the biggest loud mouth. We were now halfway down Egan's Creek with both sails drawing nicely.

It was truly magical to feel the wind drawing Echo through the water. Sailing really works. Our hand held GPS was showing six knots. This little boat can really fly I thought. At that moment we were unaware of one critical item of navigational interest. The sails appeared full and were drawing well. This couldn't explain why we were exceeding the maximum hull speed of our little boat. In my sailing bliss I was unaware that a considerable amount of our forward motion could be attributed to the ebbing tide. The ignorance of this detail only helped to heighten our enthusiasm. We were really learning to sail. As we turned out of Egan's Creek and into the main channel our speed increased even more. I attributed this increased acceleration to the freshening of the wind and my brand new sailing skills. Out in the main channel we smiled and waved to our fellow boaters with the enthusiasm of novices on our way to the ocean. They nodded back and waved. There was only one more turn coming up and we would be passing through the jetties to the sea. We made our tack.

We were running full out towards the ocean. It was then that I got my first look at the set of massive fifteen foot high buoys that mark the entrance to the St Mary's inlet.

"Wendy, get the binoculars! Why are the buoys leaning over at such a strange angle?"

Both the can and the nun were at a forty-five degree angle and the tops were pointing towards the ocean. I looked through the binoculars. It wasn't an illusion; the 2000 pound buoys were practically lying on their side.

There was so much water rushing by them that a two foot wave built up on the side facing the current and there was a big gully on the opposite side.

It was definitely time to turn around and get back in the Sound before we got sucked into the ocean. We came about. We were sailing very close to the wind and the sails were barely drawing. With a six knot current on the nose of Echo we were sailing backwards. We were coming up on the buoy at about five knots. The current was incredible. As we sailed past the buoy backwards, this gave me a very disorienting sensation. The water was pushing against the buoy so hard that we could hear a sucking, gurgling sound resonating out of the hollow buoy.

With my panic moderately under control I reached behind me and started the geriatric two cylinder Johnson outboard that I had purchased used from a local 'master mechanic'. It sputtered, coughed and revved to life. I opened the throttle up wide trying to squeeze every rpm out of her. We were ten feet from the buoy and dead in the water. We had options. We could get sucked out to sea and come back in when the tide reversed. We could beach Echo on a nearby sand bar and wait for the tide to turn. I took an alternative approach. I tacked 90 degrees to starboard and cut across the inlet to the other shore. The change in direction would give us enough wind to fight the current and take advantage of the counter current on the opposite shore. We were coming into a good position thirty feet off the shore of Cumberland Island when the engine coughed, sputtered and lost power. One of the two cylinders had blown out. Between the sails and half a motor we fought inch by inch until we were in the St Mary's channel heading into Georgian waters. We were going to be fine. We could breathe easy.

"Hey Wendy, look at those two navy tugs coming out of the sound. I wonder what they're up to."

King's Bay Submarine Base was only a couple of miles up the channel in St Mary's, Georgia. The Submarine Base is the Atlantic home port for the U.S. Navy Fleet of California Class ballistic missile nuclear submarines.

"The tugs are coming right for us" I said.

Both tugs steamed up to Echo. One held off at a distance while the other stationed ten feet off our port side. Echo was dwarfed by their size.

"Get out of the channel immediately" boomed the voice over the hailer."

I put my hands up in the air and said "I surrender. Hey if this is about that parking ticket I can explain everything."

"I'm not fooling around!" the tug captain shouted. "The sub is going to be here in a couple of minutes."

I pointed to the VHF radio in my hand. "Channel 16" I shouted. I keyed the mike. "I've got half a Johnson and the sails are pulling as much as they can. I've got a five knot current against me."

The tug captain had little interest in my Johnson. "Get out of the fairway immediately or I'm going to have to tow you out of here."

I nudged Echo closer to shore. Right then the nose of the sub came around the corner into view. The Trident submarine is an ominous monster even from a distance:

560 feet long, 42 foot beam, jet black, no markings. It looked like a giant black killer whale. The tug captain hailed me. "I have to escort the sub, stay on your course." As the sub approached to three hundred feet the whole world seemed to shrink. When the sub's bow wave hit, we were pushed sideways five feet and rocked violently. The propeller of the outboard motor came out of the water, the engine raced, coughed and died. It was beyond help. It was time to head to the dock. After the shockwave from the submarine had passed we tacked into her wake. The suction gave us a good pull back in the direction of Tiger Point.

We had been out sailing four hours. The tide was now approaching slack. We were about five miles from home with a dead motor but we were in good shape on a strong broad reach. It had been a perfect day of sailing, a little danger and excitement but no one got hurt. I wasn't going to push my luck. It would be a straight rhumb line to Egan's Creek. We were getting ready to make our tack into the channel leading to Fernandina.

"Look at all those sails" Wendy said.

The Thistle race was at its competitive climax. I was heading right for the center of the pack.

"We'll tack around them" I said to Wendy.

I looked over my shoulder and a very large freighter was making its way in through the jetties at a good clip. By the time I got to the racers I wouldn't be able to give them a proper distance and stay out of the freighter's way. I thought about dropping the sails. I was concerned that the current would push us onto a nearby sand bar. I leaned back and grabbed the tiller firmly. When we approached the fleet of Thistle racers the observers on the committee boat all stood up and started screaming and waving their arms about madly. I pressed on and cut right through the center of the race. Half the fleet went one way and half went the other. They were an aggressive lot. The first beer can cleared Wendy's head by about two feet. It then bounced off the main sail and landed in the cockpit. Two of the racers pursued us briefly, cursing and waving boat hooks.

The next day after talking with Lalia I found out that the race was a grudge match and there was more than pride, a few dollars and reputations riding on the outcome of the race. As we pulled away and distanced ourselves from the course, the racers re-organized and the race began again. Judging from this experience Thistle racers can be thornier than Trident submarines.

The tide was really starting to flood by the time we got back to Egan's creek. The current was more than five knots pushing into the creek. We had a decent wind but we were mostly getting sucked up the creek. This was the last time I made the very big mistake of following a big current into a very confined space. As the wind slackened I lost rudder control. There was more water running past the stern than the bow. The rudder was working but it was working backward.

Our slip was on the last dock on the inside, several boats from the end. The larger problem was that there was a low bridge 100 feet downstream from the marina that we would collide with if we didn't make our turn into the slip. We would have to sail past the end of the dock and make a quick 180° jibe in close quarters to get into the slip. The jibe was accidently executed flawlessly. It was the lack of wind and a swift current that started us floating backwards. I dropped the tiller, ran to the bow and tried to grab hold of one of the docked boats. I just couldn't hold Echo in the current. As we were passing the last boat on the dock, I desperately managed to get Echo's bow line tied onto a docked boat's shroud lines. I climbed aboard the docked boat and pulled Echo up one boat at a time into her slip.

I jumped onto the dock. My head was spinning. My heart was racing. Wendy and I had begun the process of learning to sail. In one short sail I took away many important lessons that stuck with me the rest of my boating life. Over the next few months Echo served us well. She was a very forgiving teacher. When there was no more that she could give us Echo was hauled, her bottom was painted and she was donated to a boy's orphanage in Jacksonville. I am sure that even today some eager young sailor is taking her out on his first sail.

Nine

Pirate Island

In the year and a half that we had owned Quest she was the center of our lives. I had spent every day lavishing her with care. In return she sustained our dreams of sailing to the Caribbean. When Quest first arrived at our home in Charlotte, NC she was both a complete mystery and an incomprehensible adventure. Quest stayed on the dry for quite some time in Charlotte. But even on the dry we derived great pleasure from building Quest into a cruising boat that was suited to our needs.

The time was near when Quest would be lowered into Egan's Creek. The only thing that was holding us back was the scarcity of slips at Tiger Point Marina. I only had two monster projects to complete before we would be ready to splash. Quest had to be re-rigged and the engine had to be overhauled. Both projects' complexity was enough to give me pause. I knew absolutely nothing about marine diesel engines. I knew even less about re-rigging a boat. All I needed was a starting point to get me out of the darkness and headed in the right direction.

The overhaul of the engine began in a quiet unplanned moment. Foster and I were sitting in the saloon with the engine hatch cover open, meditating on the Yanmar.

"This is going to be a bear to work on" I said to Foster.

He nodded and sipped his brew and took a pull on his cheroot. David Foster was a retired master sergeant in the Canadian military with 25 years experience maintaining heavy armored vehicles.

"You're not thinking about working on the engine in the boat" he said.

"You got a better idea Foster?"

"Boy, you gotta haul the engine out of the boat."

"It's that easy?" I asked.

"Sure, why not?" he said. "I'll be right back."

All six feet seven inches of Foster snapped into action. He jumped through the companionway, slid down the ladder backwards and he was gone. I laid down and was starting to nod off when I heard the travel lift start up. I didn't pay much attention until it came closer and the drumming of the lift's diesel started to shake Quest's hull. I got up to tell the lift operator that he had the wrong boat. Then I saw Foster hanging off the side of the lift yelling orders to David the operator.

"OK, leave the lift right there, we have some work to do before we're ready for you!"

Foster jumped back on Quest, grabbed the wrench set and started removing the top bolts on the motor mounts. While he disconnected the shaft coupling I worked on the hoses and wiring.

"OK Dave…go find Dave" Dave ordered.

This was a three Dave drill. Dave the operator started the engine of the lift and dropped a chain through the companionway while Dave shackled the chain to the engine pickup eye. With deliberate focus the three Daves raised the engine off the mounts. With some twisting and turning the engine cleared the hatch and was placed on blocks beside Quest.

When things calmed down a bit Foster looked at me and said "You're lucky that we hauled the engine. You've got three broken motor mounts."

Right he was. Three of the bolts were rusted and sheared. There was only one bolt holding the engine. Foster raised his hands in the air and stretched like a giant.

"You've got a lot of work ahead of you Beaupré."

He got up and started to wander in the general direction of his own boat.

"Give me a hand with this" I said.

"Nope, gotta work on my boat" he said over his shoulder. "Hey, I did all the hard work!"

The so-called easy work took about a month. The first stop was the boatyard office. With the engine manual under my arm I asked Lalia the manager if she could order Yanmar parts. She sipped her coffee.

"Yanmar parts? You must be rich. They can put a pretty good hole in your pocket" she said.

She called a friend in Jacksonville and asked him to send a price sheet. I couldn't believe the prices. It was like ordering parts for a Lamborghini.

"Don't get all worked up over the prices that you see on that list. That's retail. I'm going to get all those parts at wholesale or… maybe even a little less."

She winked. I ordered the works: pumps, hoses, oil coolers, starter, etc. I ordered replacement parts for everything that could be unbolted from the engine with the exception of the injector pump. I wasn't quite ready for open heart surgery.

The box arrived the following day.

"Where are the rest of the parts?" I asked Lalia.

"That's it baby" she said.

"That box is worth more than my car" I said.

"There you go again worrying about the price of everything. You haven't got a bill yet, have you? Now didn't I tell you that there's nothing to worry about? Go bolt those parts on before someone steals them."

I walked out of the office with a smile on my face. This was the first indication of just how much Lalia was behind our project. She soon became an official under-the-radar sponsor of our big adventure.

A diesel engine sitting on blocks in a boatyard can have magical powers of attraction. When I got to the yard the next day there were two lawn chairs sitting in front of the engine. The chairs were occupied by my friend Foster and another boatyard idler both fully engaged in caffeine induced banter. There were two more engine aficionados hovering over the Yanmar apparently attempting to take her pulse.

"You gonna work on your engine now?"

This was a highly astute group of entertainment seekers. I dug in the back of my car and pulled out the box of parts and placed it gingerly on the ground. I looked over at Foster and told him to grab the ½ inch socket and start taking off the oil pan.

"Sorry man I'm busy."

I looked at the rest of the crowd and asked for volunteers.

"Gotta get to work, sorry."

"I gotta go to the hardware store."

Within thirty seconds the place cleared out. It was time to dig in and get greasy.

My parts replacement strategy was simple and conservative. I unbolted an old part. I cleaned it, oiled it and placed it in a dry plastic bag with a packet of silica gel. The old parts then went into a locker on Quest as spares. The new part was bolted and tightened. Foster was sure right about one thing. There was no way that I could have done the job without hauling the engine. Bolt by bolt all the new parts were installed and five coats of engine paint were sprayed on. It looked better than a new engine.

Foster and I were sitting beside the engine watching the paint dry and planning how we were going to test start the Yanmar one morning when Lalia came out of the office. She called me aside.

"Have you run the engine yet?"

"No."

"Is it going to run OK?"

"I don't see why not. Why are you asking?"

"There's a betting pool on your engine."

"Is there anything that these guys won't bet on?"

"No."

"What are the odds?" I asked.

"Three to one."

For a fleeting moment my ego was indulged. I nodded my head and smiled with self satisfaction.

"Ah…no…three to one" she repeated. "Three to one that you are going to flop."

I was properly deflated.

"Can I get in on the bet?" I asked.

"Of course not silly, that would be illegal. Just don't start the engine until tomorrow around 9:30 in the morning!"

"I'll start it tomorrow at exactly 9:30" I said.

Foster and I scrambled to get everything ready for the next day. The hardware store was stocked with the essentials: diesel jerry can, hoses, and jumper wires. We were sitting in front of the Yanmar by 8:00 the next morning as ready as we would ever be when Lalia strode over nonchalantly.

"OK, here are the rules. The engine has to be cold, it has to start within the first ten seconds, so once you start cranking don't stop. It also has to run for at least ten minutes."

"Sounds good" I said.

By 9:00 a small crowd had gathered. The crowd grew into a shoulder to shoulder ring of gamblers encircling the Yanmar at about twenty feet. Every so often one of the spectators would walk up to the Yanmar and feel the top of the engine to confirm that she was cold. I told Foster to go and tell Lalia that we were ready. I primed the engine for the third time. The crowd was getting rowdy.

"OK Dave" I said. "Start the water."

He turned on the garden hose. Water poured out from the mixing elbow at the back of the engine. I reached across the battery and energized the starter wire. The engine gave out two big 'woo…woos' and started up with a deafening unmuffled diesel throb and ran for the obligatory ten minutes. Fifteen minutes later and the show was over. I looked over at the porch of the office where five burly shrimpers reluctantly slammed currency onto Lalia's palm. She looked over at me with a thumbs up and a very satisfied Cheshire cat grin.

With the Yanmar tested and properly installed it was time to tackle the job of re-rigging Quest. The thought of me cutting, splicing and tuning my own rigging gave my boatyard neighbors the shivers. I gave everyone the same answer when they told me that I was crazy. 'So, you think that I should find a rigger that I don't know and I don't trust and pay him a fortune?' I shouldn't have been surprised when the most common reply was 'Of course'. The only person that was completely opposed to me paying a rigger was Foster.

"Don't worry about those children. They don't know squat. They can't even pump their own gas. Get Brion Toss's video."

"Who's Brion Toss?" I asked.

"He's a real celebrity rigger from the left coast. He's got a bunch of DYI videos about how to do everything. I think he's even got one on how to fry an egg in boiling sea water. Wait a minute."

He threw me down a package. It was titled 'Tuning Your Rig' by Brion Toss. When I got home I played it through with Wendy. When she got bored I played it again for the cats. I was confident that with a good wire tension gauge I could rig Quest. My confidence faltered a bit when the delivery driver rolled the 150 pound spool of Dyform rigging wire off the back of the truck and tossed me the 25 pound box of swageless terminals and assorted fittings. I brought the box into the living room. I was completely overwhelmed. I stared at it. I was completely over my head I thought. But with the terminals and fittings laid out systematically on the floor arranged as they would be installed on Quest the process seemed manageable.

Most of the standing rigging was over fifty feet in length. We needed a very long, dry covered space to measure and cut the wire and make up the Norseman fittings. The only place that I could think of was Tiger Point's pavilion. I approached Captain K, the boatyard owner, the following day to see if he would agree. Captain K's flinty personality was highly unpredictable. The neighborhood stray dogs and cats as well as a good portion of the marina's clientele avoided getting any closer to him than fifty feet. He was driven and blind-sided by self interest.

"Hey Captain K, can I use the pavilion to splice some rigging?"

"Yeah, sure, you can use the building" he said. "Don't make a mess and be out of there by the race Sunday. Those racers haven't forgotten about you breaking up the race last season! Hey, by the way your slip is ready. I am going to start billing you from today. That's just a little incentive to get you off your ass and get the boat in the water. You can thank me later. By the way it's a really great slip."

He pointed to a vacant spot at the dock.

"I'll go take a look later" I said.

"You do that" he replied.

Several hours later the last piece of wire was cut from the spool. Eight pieces of wire lay on the pavilion floor ready to be made up into stays, shrouds and bobstay. Wendy and I had a good days work ahead of us to make up the swages.

This seemed like a good time to take a look at our new slip assignment. I walked out on the dock thinking that Captain K had showed me uncharacteristic kindness in giving me such a choice slip. As I got within twenty feet of the slip I thought that I was seeing some kind of optical illusion. Then a cold shiver went through me. The tide was in full ebb. Four inches of creek mud was showing above the water line. Quest has a 6 foot draft. This wasn't a slip, it was a parking space. I stormed back to the office to confront Captain K.

"Where is he?" I said to Lalia.

"Easy does it now. I know that Captain K stiffed you with the bad slip, but just calm down."

"I'm going to be a lot calmer after I kill Captain K!" I said.

"That's not quite calm enough. Sit down." She lit a cigarette and sat down beside me. "You can go out hunting for Captain K. Good luck. If you cause a big enough stink

The rig was statically tuned. Dyform wire is an architectural wire that doesn't need re-tensioning. This was as far as I could take Quest on dry land. The most important step in tuning the rig would be to bring Quest out on the water, heel her over and dynamically tune the shrouds when there was maximum pressure on the wire. But first things first, I would have to get Quest onto the water.

I was admiring my handiwork and wondering whether I would ever see Quest at the dock when Lalia came over.

"Hey, she looks like a sailboat now" she said. "Do you remember that slip I told you about a week ago?"

"Of course I remember."

"Look over there" Lalia said.

Dr. Jacobs was warming up his engine. Within fifteen minutes he cast off his lines and was gone.

"There's your new slip, just like I promised. It's the best in the marina."

This was definitely a great slip. It was at the end of a long hundred foot dock. I had the slip for the real beginner. I could come and go at any tide with no tricky side docking maneuvers even in a five knot current. Best of all, the currents wouldn't give me the cold sweats.

Quest was scheduled to be picked up and splashed first thing Monday morning at slack tide.

Ten

The Splash

For the last two years, Quest had been on the hard. But even on land she was full of surprises. If all went well Quest would soon be putting the land to her stern and beginning a new life on the ocean. Splashing a boat in Egan's Creek was a challenge for even the most experienced boater. The travel slip was positioned 90° to a tidal stream that flowed at five to six knots. I had seen many boaters underestimate the power of the current with calamitous results. With a side current of this magnitude the only practical time to launch or haul a boat in the creek was at full high or low tide.

When Captain K, the owner of the boatyard, got wind that Lalia and I had hoodwinked him out of the best slip in the marina, he took it like a man.

"Beaupré, you've got 24 hours to get your boat in that slip."

"I'm waiting on my shaft coupling. It's on back order" I said.

"In 24 hours you're slip will be on backorder. You have 24 hours."

Quest and Crew

"Can you splash Quest tomorrow morning at high tide and help me over to the slip with the pilot boat?" I asked.

"Don't worry" he said. "You'll get into your slip." One quickly learns in Fernandina that the expression 'don't worry' is the cornerstone of the local vernacular. It serves the same purpose that the adjustable wrench serves in shade-tree mechanics. Just as the all purpose adjustable wrench has stripped the head off many a bolt, the expression 'don't worry' has brought many a situation to a bad end. I was far too easily taken in by the reassuring resonance of Captain K's 'don't worry.'

The following morning was a fine day to splash Quest. The wind was low, the temperature perfect. The haul was scheduled for 08:30. Wendy and I were at the boatyard waiting for Captain K by 07:30. Quest was unblocked and in the slings by 08:00 and on her way to the travel slip. By 08:30 every thing was proceeding without a hitch. We had nothing to worry about. Quest was in the slings poised over Egan's Creek ready to be launched.

Captain K revved the lift and slowly lowered Quest into the muddy creek water. It was my personal moment of truth. Had I bedded all those new through-hulls, hoses and transducers correctly, would the new dripless packing gland leak? Would the two large Dynaplates hold water? This was definitely not the time for reflection. For an experienced hand this would have been just another day. Quest's owner was showing all the signs of being a first timer. My palms were sweating. My heart was racing. I dashed from bow to stern and checked every inch of the bilge for leaks. I waited. I rechecked it all a second time. All the while Captain K stood leaning against the superstructure of the lift shouting at me to "speed it up."

"OK, it looks like everything is ready" I said.

Captain K stepped back onto the lift.

"So how are you getting over to your slip?" he asked.

"You're taking us over with the pilot boat."

"No I'm not" he said. My first thought was that he was just having a little fun at my expense.

"I believe you agreed to tow Quest over to the dock" I said.

"No. No, I didn't say anything of the kind. This tide is coming up fast. If you don't pull out of the slip soon then I'll have to haul and block your boat before it gets jammed against the lift. I've got to think about my travel lift! You have one hour. And by the way if you don't haul today I am giving the slip away to a friend of mine."

Oh, that's what this is all about. I walked over to the office and sat on a bench on the porch to regain my equanimity. I had been blind sided. If I had been a little more wary of Captain K's motives then I could have avoided this situation. Quest was proving to be a most versatile teacher. At first glance she was only a beautiful cruising boat. She was now providing poignant lessons into how spiteful someone could really be.

At the most, this inconvenient situation would cost a few hundred dollars. It was the loss of the slip that would turn this problem into a calamity. Lalia sat beside me on the porch and started to laugh.

"So this is funny?" I asked.

"Don't worry" she laughed.

"Don't worry? Don't worry? I think I should worry!"

"Well worry if you have to, just don't panic. He's already on his way."

"Who's on his way?"

"Jackson will be here in 15 minutes."

"Who's Jackson?"

"Jackson's a friend of mine. He's coming down to tow Quest to her slip. I called him a couple of days ago and had him stand by. When K found out that I assigned you that slip he turned red in the face and let out a low growling sound. I kinda figured that he would try and pull something. I can't really say that I blame him."

When Jackson motored up, he tied off to the travel lift pier in front of Quest. There wasn't a second to waste. I located Captain K working on an outboard engine by the tool shed.

"You ready to call it a day Beaupré?"

"Can you start up the lift?" I asked.

Captain K scratched the back of his head and gave me a self satisfied grin.

"Don't feel bad Beaupré. I knew I had you when I drove in today."

He started off in the general direction of the Travel Lift. Then he spotted the skiff tied off to the Travel Lift slip.

"Lalia, what's Jackson doing tied off to the Travel Lift slip?"

The Splash

"Oh good, he finally showed up" she said. "He's here to tow Quest into her new slip."

Captain K balled up the rag that he was using to wipe the grease from his hands. He wound up and gave the rag a dramatic fast pitch at the office door. The rag hit about five feet up the door with a thud then slowly slid to the floor leaving a greasy smudge where it had made contact. All spectators abandoned the porch.

"Come on, let's get your boat in the water. The tide is coming up fast" he said.

The water was coming up fast. Captain K didn't have to lower Quest much to free her from the slings. With a good pull from Jackson on Quest's bow line we were out in the stream. Even Jackson underestimated the force of the current. Within seconds Quest was being pushed downstream sideways. With Jackson in front of Quest, it was impossible for him to slow her down.

"Throw out your anchor" he yelled.

"The anchor?" I said.

"Yeah, throw it out. Throw it out."

"It should be here sometime next week" I said.

Jackson threw back his head and gave out a big laugh. He reached to the stern and released the slack line that was between Quest's bow and his stern.

"Ready a line on your stern" he shouted.

A moment later he had motored along side Quest. He tied off both lines and then engaged his engine in one smooth motion. In what seemed to me like the seamless action of a master at the helm he took up the slack in the towing line and checked Quest's drift down the creek.

Quest and Crew

We edged to the dock slowly where Lalia and Wendy were standing to catch our lines. With the dock lines secured, we were enveloped in a brief moment of good cheer and congratulations. Then the party was over before it got started. Lalia was off to the marina office and Wendy to the apartment. Calmness returned after several hours of logistic uncertainty. I was alone again in the cockpit with a cup of warm tea in my hand. The wonderful silence of Egan's Creek was more than adequate to underscore the successes of the past two years. But as always, at these short moments of savored victory, my mind drifted to the next time that Quest would require intervention. I was blissfully engaged in a continuing adventure in which Wendy and I served as Quest's stewards.

During the two day hiatus while waiting for the shaft coupling to be delivered, I remained fully entertained by the wonderful variety of life forms that populated the marsh. There were birds that dined exclusively on crabs at low tide and others that preferred the daintier side orders of bugs and slithering things that abound in the marsh. When the six foot tide flooded the marsh, a vast army of fowl descended on the creek to devour the fish that were pushed in from the ocean. But of particular interest were the large water mammals. Each day like clock work a small pod of dolphins came up the creek at high tide to forage. Every day they would silently come along side Quest and then without warning let loose with a roaring chorus of dolphin squeals. They were always playful and curious while at the same time wary of human activity.

The Splash

My first introduction to the manatee was a very welcome surprise. The day after the courier delivered my shaft coupling I was deep in the bilge when I heard a scraping sound on the hull. With the amount of debris that floated up and down the creek in the swift current, a bang or thump on the hull was not out of the ordinary. But in the confined space of the bilge the sounds were greatly magnified. When the banging turned into a constant scraping I imagined that an object had wedged between the boat and dock. I finished the coupling installation and jumped on the dock. I reached down into the creek up to my shoulder and felt along Quest's hull to dislodge the debris. Suddenly beside my head an enormous 'demon of the deep' surfaced inches from my hand and started making for my fingers. I pulled back rapidly and rolled over on the dock. When I looked up, Nash the owner of the sport fishing boat next to Quest was watching and thoroughly enjoying the show.

"Hey don't worry it's just a manatee" he said. "They are about as friendly as it gets. Give it some fresh water from that garden hose."

I turned on the hose beside Quest and placed the nozzle in the water. The manatee took the hose in its mouth and drank hardily.

"That's enough; just give him a little taste. And never ever feed them! Hey, if the Government wildlife people see you messing with the manatee you'll find out just how dangerous wildlife can be."

So there was Quest tied to the dock in Egan's Creek. She was recommissioned and shinier than a new penny. She had an uncommon ability to attract attention. Attracting attention at this time is not what I was looking for. It seemed that everyone had their own particular view about how I should handle the docking of Quest. Everyone was most generous with advice. It seemed that my particular circumstance was all the provocation that the local boating populace needed to inundate me with unsolicited advice. Unsolicited or not, all of these minor treatises on boating procedure usually appeared to contain at least a nugget or two of gold, the luster of which was often impermanent. After thorough consideration and painful extraction of all valuables, a sizable cache was accumulated consisting largely of unusable information. By far the most poignant nugget of unsolicited advice was offered by Captain K. "This creek is no place for a beginner to learn to dock a full keel sailboat." Captain K's candor was most appropriate; Captain K's comment was also an unusable nugget.

My greatest pool of knowledge came from the observation of the casual minded boater attempting a docking at Tiger Point. These weekend boaters were in a powerful rush to relax. This casual approach gave birth to the term 'collision docking' a term that could be used with great frequency on a Sunday afternoon.

I had developed a healthy respect for the incomprehensible nature of the creek. Ready or not, it was now time to take on the responsibility of learning the basics of docking. A new endeavor of such mechanical complexity requires live simulation. Simulation was necessary in our case to isolate all unforeseen shortcomings and at the same time to build Wendy and me into a well coordinated docking machine. For several days we simulated arrivals and departures at a variety of tide stages. For several days we endured the good natured taunts from our neighbors. 'You have to let the lines go if you ever want to get anywhere!' 'Captain K better not catch you trying to steal that dock!' Before long, docking procedures were developed and refined. We were ready to cast off.

With a proper shove off the dock, we eased into the current. With my heart pounding I reached into the winch locker for a dry shop rag and wiped the cold sweat off the wheel. Before we had made it the quarter of a mile down Egan's Creek I was beginning to get the feel for steering Quest. Compared to our training on our tiny sailboat Echo, Quest was a real pleasure to steer. Her long deep keel removed any tendency to crab or veer off course.

We had a long list of things to accomplish on our maiden voyage. I had added a completely new high tech instrument package just before we splashed so the first bit of business was to do a full calibration of the system. By the time we got to the Cumberland Sound all of the new electronic toys were fully operational and giving us what we could assume were good readings with the one exception of the compass transducer. The setup for the compass was a study in the obtuse. The manual read 'While motoring a circle with a radius of no less than a quarter of a mile and at a speed of no more than three knots, press the on/off button twice within five seconds, then hold down the on/off button and the page up button simultaneously for one complete revolution of the circle. The display will blink on and off twice. When the display blinks twice the compass is fully calibrated.' It seemed straight forward.

The first time around the circle I inadvertently took my hand off the display to make a course correction. The second time around I believe that I didn't press the buttons simultaneously enough or I only pressed the on/off button once. I just couldn't get the display to blink twice. Around and around the Sound we went. We were on our fifth trip when the Coast Guard patrol boat came out of the Port of Fernandina docks and made straight for us. We were still making circles when he came alongside and requested a tie up. I cut the engines and tied him alongside. A most serious young Coast Guard officer came to his gunwales and asked us if we had called for a tow yet.

"A tow?" I said. "A tow for what?"

"The Fernandina harbor pilot hailed us to report a boat in distress in the middle of the Sound. He told us he suspected a jammed rudder. He's got a ship coming in and he needs you to get out of the fairway."

"We are setting our compass" I said.

"You're doing what?"

"We're calibrating the compass. You know you steer a circle about a half of a mile wide and you press this button twice then you hold down these two buttons."

By no stretch of the imagination was he a gadget guru.

"OK, sure whatever. If you don't need any help cast me off."

While I was reaching over to throw him the line I said "When you get back to town make sure that you thank

The Splash

Captain K for me. Tell him that it was most considerate to
send you boys out to help us."

"Will do" he said. "Are you going to be going
around in circles much longer?"

"No officer. We are just about done here."

Two more trips around the Sound and the compass
was properly calibrated. This was the moment we were
waiting for. The wind had freshened to fifteen knots. I
raised the main and headsails. I don't think that I will ever
forget the first time that I raised the main on Quest. The
characteristic crisp snap of a re-resined sail filled with wind
gave me goose bumps. Quest isn't a performer in low wind
but come fifteen knots she will fly. There was plenty of
room in the Sound to practice every point of sail. We even
briefly had both head sails up wing on wing. It was a
perfect day and a perfect sail.

Our final challenge for this perfect day would be to
give the new windlass and anchor a good workout. We
sailed up in the lee of a barrier island and dropped the
hook. There was something about the theory of anchoring
that I just couldn't fully absorb. With no experience to
guide me, I couldn't comprehend how a 55 pound chunk of
steel could hold a boat that weighed ten tons in a current
that was exceeding five knots. I knew the theory well
enough. I knew how a plow anchor engaged the bottom
and how the chain's catenary held it at the correct angle. It
just took one good practical demonstration to convince me.

We were in about twenty feet of water when I let
the anchor go. When the anchor hit bottom we started to
drift back. When we came to the end of the 120 feet of

115

chain that I had let out Quest stopped dead and snapped to attention and the chain went bar tight.

This was all so new. For two people anchored off Cumberland Island this was the initiation into an odyssey that would carry us to places that we couldn't even imagine. We sat in the cockpit, dined and spoke of the future. But the tide was turning slack. It wouldn't be long before the marshes would be giving their flood water back to the ocean. We just had time to clean up, haul the anchor and make our way to the dock. If everything worked as planned we would come up to the dock with a three knot current right on the nose. We hoisted the sails and made slow progress tacking in a head wind across the Sound until we reached Egan's Creek.

A day as good as this wouldn't be complete without at least one reminder of the fickle nature of the currents in Egan's Creek. While I was making my way up the creek I had to make an abrupt course change to avoid a floating log. It was then that Quest swung broad side to the current and bolted for the shore of the creek. She wouldn't answer the helm. At least she refused to go where I wanted to go. I aborted my docking attempt, spun Quest around and proceeded back down the creek toward the Sound. By the time I got out to the main channel to turn around and wipe the sweat off the wheel I was certain what I had done wrong. The current had caught the keel and rotated her sideways. The only remedy that I could see for this type of problem was to keep as straight as possible in the current.

I entered the creek again and started my approach. I was determined to keep Quest on a relatively straight path.

The Splash

Wendy was standing at the boarding ladder, docking lines in hand. I motored slowly up to the dock until Quest's midship was within inches of the dock. Wendy jumped ashore and tied the bow line to the dock cleat. I gave Quest a little reverse and Wendy secured the stern line. We had made a perfect docking on our very first attempt. Not every subsequent docking would be so perfect.

Our small docking success did not go unnoticed. Nash had just discharged his paying guests from his boat following a full day of deep sea fishing. They were milling about the dock examining the catch of the day when we made our docking approach. When we finally got our spring line cleated off the entire group gave us a rousing round of applause. One of the more outgoing members of the group walked over to us and said he wanted to shake my hand.

"This isn't the first time this guy's docked a boat!" he said to the crowd.

I thanked him for the compliment and looked over at Nash who was sporting a full grin on his face. Wendy and I collected our gear and walked up the dock to the parking lot. When we were out of ear shot of Nash's guests we both looked at each other and doubled over with laughter.

See photographs of Fernandina Beach
at www.questandcrew.com

Eleven

Hello, North Palm Beach

"**G**ood morning Parker Bridge, this is the sailing vessel Quest requesting an opening."

"Roger Quest, I see your approach. Go to full throttle. We can't keep these drivers waiting. This is road rage Monday. I've already been hit by two cappuccinos and a bear claw" joked the bridge operator.

"I'm going to full throttle. Thanks for the opening Parker Bridge. Quest out."

As we passed under the bascule bridge the sun glinted off the tinted windshields of a long line of BMW's, Jaguars and Bentleys that stretched for a quarter of a mile. Parker Bridge was our fifth and last opening of that morning. All five bridges were over busy highways on a six mile stretch of the Intracoastal Waterway (ICW). The off hand comments from the bridge operators that morning left no room for doubt. We were no longer in Fernandina Beach. We had just arrived in North Palm Beach after enjoying our leisurely trip down the ICW from Fernandina. We would be making a big change in our lifestyle. We would now take up residence as live aboard cruisers at Old Port Cove in Lake Worth, home of the well heeled winter residents from the Northeast boroughs. We were booked in for a year at OPC. This would give us the time to put the final touches on Quest and develop our blue water sailing skills before leaving for the Caribbean.

Just three short weeks prior to our arrival in North Palm we were docked at Tiger Point Marina in Fernandina Beach finalizing our preparations for our excursion down the ICW. With the tanks topped off, provisions aboard and beer ballast secured, we said good bye to the friends and acquaintances who had witnessed our progression from profoundly inexperienced boaters to fully inexperienced live aboard cruisers. There is no test, no government license, and no sanctioning society that bestows the title of live aboard cruiser. The entrance fee is a boat that can be generally kept above the water line and a willingness to accept less than ideal living conditions. The requirement necessary to make someone a genuine live aboard is a lack of fixed address. 'Oh yes, we live on our boat. No, I can't really tell you where we will be next week.' But to become a successful live aboard cruiser, to live on a boat year after year and retain a facsimile of sanity, requires the reshaping of personality and a change in values.

The success rate of cruisers staying on their boat for a minimum of one year is very low. Every first time cruiser begins with high hopes. The failure rate among this group of adventurers is not usually the result of boat accidents, deaths, injury or financial difficulties. People leave the cruising life in the first year because they simply find that the lifestyle is a bad fit from the start. This can be a very tough lesson to learn. We have usually found that the failed inductee is never short of believable excuses. "My children just can't live without me." "Little Muffin our shih tzu just can't hold her water that long." "My brother's roses in Toronto have aphids." When failure takes a back seat to pride any excuse sounds better than the truth. "What do you mean we can't keep ice cream hard?" "Does the head always smell like that?" When new cruisers 'swallow the anchor' it's usually the head or the galley that begins the systematic spiral of discomfort in the lifestyle. Being forewarned of these fatal pitfalls I spared no expense in either of these vital areas.

As we pushed off the dock and into the ebbing tide of Egan's Creek for the last time we waved to the small group of friends that had gathered. When we stepped on board that morning we started a long partnership with Quest. In the next four years we would only spend a total of 27 days away from Quest. When we had motored the quarter of a mile to the end of the creek and made our turn into the ICW I glanced around to take one last look. The owner of the marina, Captain K, had also been anticipating our departure. Always pragmatic the good Captain had already launched a boat from storage and was in the process of placing her in our old slip.

"Do you think he's trying to tell us something?" Wendy asked.

"I think he is making himself perfectly clear. Don't hurry back, y'all."

With the 350 mile cruise down to North Palm Beach ahead of us, the memory of Tiger Point was put away. The first and immediate goal of our newborn adventure would be to anchor off the city of Fernandina Beach and experience an aspect of the town entirely new to us. We would spend the night like so many before us. We were just two of the many boaters passing through a small industrial town on the ICW on their way to south Florida.

There are two ways to get from North Palm Beach to Fernandina by water. In the autumn an intrepid sailor can sail down the coast of Florida, fighting a five knot Gulf Stream, head winds and frequent squalls for the entire three hundred and fifty miles. In a big hurry it can be done in several days. It was the peak of hurricane season. We were not intrepid. We were definitely not in a hurry. Motoring the ICW from the Georgia border to South Florida is a veritable study in hydrology, ecology and sociology. The two latter 'ologies' added the necessary recreational distraction for our first extended cruise. The real time application of hydrology provided the 'edge of the seat' thrills.

The most basic description of the ICW is a canal comprised of naturally occurring creeks, lakes, and sounds behind barrier islands linked together by dredged canals. Although the ICW is used extensively by pleasure boaters its original purpose was the commercial movement of barge traffic up and down the coast. The controlled depth of the ICW is eight feet. By no means should this be misconstrued as a guaranteed depth. The depth in areas subject to shoaling can be four feet, just enough water for a tug to push an oil barge over the sand bar but two feet short of floating Quest. As they say in Fernandina 'if you haven't grounded a few times you haven't been out sailing much'. There are better ways to learn to stay off the mud flats than grounding every Sunday afternoon.

I was raised in the Niagara Peninsula. The spring is a very rainy time of year. There was never a day that I didn't look forward to going out in the rain and playing in one of the many swollen creeks. Working my way up from the age of four at the helm of floating leaves and sticks, I successfully honed my skills so that I could easily navigate a good sized chunk of log down any overflowing stream in my immediate watershed. All river navigation after that was just a matter of scale and technique. The skills necessary to navigate the ICW were those learned in rubber boots at a tender age. The ICW is just another muddy creek. Possessing this native ability for the subtleties of hydrology predisposed me to make a very erroneous assumption. What I failed to realize was that Wendy did not possess any natural ability for river piloting.

The anchor was raised and Fernandina put to stern before the smoke belching pulp plant sounded the siren for the morning shift change. Were we really leaving all this behind for the blue water paradise of South Florida? The first novel experience of the day was to make our first passage under the fixed bridge connecting the island with the mainland. At mid tide there was about sixty-five feet from the water to the bottom of the bridge. This gave us a mere eight feet clearance to the top of the mast and three feet to the VHF antenna. From the cockpit the illusion of the mast hitting the bridge was real enough to make us both duck. Motoring under fixed bridges was a small concern in comparison to the extremely winding stretch of river that lay before us from Fernandina to the Nassau Sound.

After we passed under the Amelia Island Bridge I asked Wendy to take the wheel briefly. I had a pot of cereal cooking on the stove that needed a stir. My last words to Wendy were "Watch the buoys". I had just opened the pot. The lid of the pot was in one hand and spoon in the other when Quest came to an abrupt jarring stop. I was thrown forward. The spoon in my hand ricocheted off the cabin ceiling and landed on the settee. The lid was catapulted forward and came to rest in the stateroom. Had we collided with another boat or a buoy? I climbed up the companionway and was immediately assaulted by Wendy's fear induced monologue.

"I don't know what happened. The boat just stopped. I didn't hit anything. The boat just stopped. I did exactly like you told me. I went straight from buoy to buoy. See, we're right between the buoys."

We were indeed directly between the two buoys. We were also clearly out of the channel.

"You don't steer buoy to buoy. The idea here is to stay in the channel. The buoys are there to tell you where the shoals are."

No amount of profanity was going to raise Quest off the bottom that morning. The only event that aided in lowering the exchange of invectives between Wendy and me was the approach of a crab boat and its crew of two. International marine law dictates that whenever a boater manages to display extremely poor judgment there has to be a witness. The crabbers took one look at Quest and went stiff backed and straight faced. On passing they both looked over in unison and gave us their full attention, demonstrating their above average repertoire of smirks and nods. There was no offer of assistance. Grounding in five feet of water put us beyond the help of these boys. When they had motored fifty feet beyond Quest they both broke out in laughter, swerved their boat a couple of times, nearly hitting a buoy before recovering their composure. The tide was rising so it was just a matter of time before we would be underway. We sat in the cockpit, ate breakfast, and washed the dishes. We sat a while longer until we finally felt Quest ease off the mud and begin to float down the stream.

During breakfast I digested the charts for Nassau Sound. Nassau Sound is reputed to be one of the most challenging navigational hazards in North Florida. While we lived in Fernandina at least one sailboat a week grounded on its boat-eating sand bars. A good number of these grounded boats spent days sitting on the bottom while crews struggled to free them. Even on a perfect day there is a 90 ° course change one hundred feet before a low fixed bridge. The channel after the course change is very narrow and shallow with shifting shoals. The current that hits a transiting boat full broad side is strong enough to easily nudge an unwary captain out of the channel and into trouble. On a paper chart it looked deceptively easy. I studied the charts, the distances, vectors, buoy location. It was time for the final exam.

We were about a half mile from Nassau Sound when I first spotted the squall line. Against the deep blue sky the squall line was midnight black. North Florida can generate squalls of considerable intensity. This storm was about to cut across Nassau Sound. It looked bad. Should I be in the narrow channel of the ICW or should I get out in the Sound where I would have more room to maneuver?

"Get your rain gear on right now!" I yelled to Wendy.

As I suited up, Quest was coming out of the creek and her nose was just beginning to poke into the Sound. The contrast between the brilliantly sunlit Sound and the approaching squall line was frightening. I lined Quest up on her new course dead straight for the buoy. The opaque squall line was racing towards us at thirty knots. The first raindrops began to beat off the hard top. The wind freshened to forty knots. The rain came in torrents.

Screaming to be heard, I turned to Wendy "Take the wheel. I have to go to the bow to spot the buoy. Stay exactly on this course, exactly. This should bring Quest within five feet of the buoy. When Quest's stern clears the buoy make your 90° course change."

I recognized well after the fact that although I was aware that the 90° turn was to starboard, Wendy was not so informed.

The storm's intensity increased. I could barely make out Quest's forward pulpit through the wall of water. I stepped onto the catwalk and crawled my way to the bow. By the time that I had gotten to the bow the cockpit had disappeared. Wendy was using an accurate digital compass so I knew that she would stay on course. My greatest concern was the force of the wind and current striking hard of starboard. The engine was at full throttle and we were only making two and a half knots. Even at that speed we seemed to be taking much too long to reach the buoy. With visibility at less than five feet, missing the buoy was a real possibility. If we missed the buoy and continued without the 90° course change we would hit the low fixed bridge before we had time to react.

When I first spotted the buoy it seemed to just appear out of the storm off Quest's starboard bow. Wendy had found her target. We still weren't in the clear. Hand over hand, I pulled my way along the deck as fast as I could and jumped into the cockpit.

"Course change, 90° now!" I shouted.

Wendy started swinging the wheel to port. Watching in complete disbelief I shouted "No!" I grabbed one side of the wheel. Wendy clenched the other side with both hands. For one tense moment the two of us engaged in a surreal struggle for control of the helm with a raging storm circling around us. There was no time for discussion. I shoved Wendy well clear of the wheel. The buoy was just starting to disappear behind me. I swung Quest a full 90° starboard. Wendy regained her footing and began screaming.

"You're going the wrong direction. Turn the other way."

I can't even begin to imagine the fear and anxiety that the ambiguity in our course must have caused her. She was unaware that her course was 180° in the wrong direction. She was certain that we were about to crash at any moment. She sat down resigned to her mistaken belief that we were about to hit the bridge. The storm began to abate but I still couldn't see the next buoy on the opposite shore of the Sound. I was steering a vector blindly based solely on what I remembered from reading the chart. Like many squalls in North Florida it was over faster than it started. When we reached the Sound's midpoint the storm had passed and sunlight lit up the next south bound buoy on the opposite side of the Sound.

The storm had come on us so quickly and disappeared with such speed that it all seemed like a dream. We had successfully threaded the needle of Nassau Sound in a blinding squall. We both sat silently as we motored south thinking about the event. When we reached our anchorage that night a lot of the tension had faded.

When we spoke of the incident we were astounded at how differently the experience had affected us. 'Grounding and a near mishap in the matter of one hour' I thought. Would I have to deal with this or worse every day? This was a challenging prospect. It might be a little more challenge than I had bargained for. Wendy on the other hand had a profound moment of truth. The events of the day had forced her to realize that she was essential to our success. She was determined to be a dedicated crew member. The seriousness of her pledge was enough to breathe new life into our dubious venture. Wendy was thus and with little ceremony promoted from the lowest rank of scupper to cub river boat pilot. By the time we arrived in North Palm Wendy had piloted the ever changing ICW without further incident.

What could be written about the ICW that hasn't already been written? There is enough description, elaboration, exaggeration and bad poetry printed to completely fill in the ICW from New Jersey to Miami. With the prospects of unintentional plagiarism being a real possibility my description of the ICW will be as brief as possible.

Beginning at Fernandina Beach the ICW is dotted with small towns, each with surprisingly rich history. Like Fernandina, St. Augustine claims to be the oldest city in America. This rivalry persists even today largely due to the fact that most of the eyewitnesses are not above ground. So down the ICW we motored and motor sailed, miles of crooked creeks and miles of straight dredged channels. Palm Coast, Daytona Beach, each city attempting to outdo the next in spending their town's resources to create a delightful waterfront façade where the boater will feel at ease and encouraged to spend freely. New Smyrna Beach, Cocoa, Vero Beach: each city provides good anchorage, plentiful local color and considerable individuality. Sail boaters will naturally find themselves at ease in these slower paced towns.

But your leisure is about to be usurped. You are about to cross the border into South Florida where the sailboat is about as welcome as barnacles on a prop. Stuart Florida is where the imaginary line between sail and power is drawn. With their numbers swelled to unimaginable ranks the power boaters, intoxicated on gasoline fumes and emblazoned by speed, consider it their personal duty to make it as uncomfortable for the sail boater as possible. Ever since the Yamahas, Evinrudes and the big Johnsons moved into South Florida there has been a friendly competition among power boaters. Points are assigned to power boat captains for all conceivable assaults on the unsuspecting sail boater. The creativity and thoughtlessness of an assault solely determines its value when assigning points. One point is accumulated for a customary high speed pass of a sailboat in a no wake zone. Ten points can be earned for a full cockpit drenching. As points are accumulated they can be redeemed at your favorite fuel dock for prizes and bragging rights.

Stuart extends a hearty welcome to the powerboat industry. It also serves as a contrast to North Florida. This is where the muddy chocolate waters of North Florida turn magically into the remarkably blue waters of South Florida. It is also on this stretch of former barge canal that the unoccupied multi-million dollar cottages begin to line the ICW all the way to Miami like a gaudy necklace.

From Stuart to North Palm Beach the pace of our journey accelerated. A notable reason for this change to our snail like advance down the ICW was the necessity to avoid no anchoring zones. These highly controversial no anchoring zones, although totally without any legal legitimacy and contrary to Federal law, serve the express interest of the aforementioned property owners. Their rights are dutifully enforced by the best local law enforcement that money can buy.

We passed under Parker Bridge and made our turn into Lake Worth. We were in no hurry to have our first outing come to an end. We were trying our best to drag it out as long as we could. It was due entirely to the insistence of five bridge operators that we kept our speed up that morning. Traveling from our home on laid back Amelia Island for 350 miles to the hectic pace of South Florida in a mere three weeks left us with culture shock worthy of intercontinental travel. But in some ways we were looking forward to our new dockage at Old Port Cove and beginning our new life as live aboard cruisers. We had only one short year before the end of next year's hurricane season. Then it would be time to leave Old Port Cove for the Bahamas; one year to put the finishing touches on Quest. More importantly we had one year to become blue water sailors.

Twelve

Zero G

I admit that there is a certain optimistic naivety in thinking that Wendy and I could become blue water cruisers. Yes, we were completely inexperienced. But we were not unprepared. My action plan, if it could be misconstrued as a plan, consisted of a play book with far fewer answers than questions. These blank spaces would in due course be filled in as we proceeded south from South Florida to the Caribbean. I was certain that experience would catch up with us at some point. No plan is perfect. Some plans are stymied in their germination. Before experience had a chance to find me, my greatest nemesis clenched me in its iron jaws, refused my plea for mercy and nearly slammed the door shut on our sailing adventure.

Seasickness, this enemy of mine and friend to no one, gained access to Quest while we were on a routine sail and equipment shakedown in the Gulf Stream. I had spent the previous week acquainting myself and installing that magical piece of gear poetically referred to as a water maker. For sailors wishing to spend their days on deserted palm fringed tropical islands reverse osmosis desalination will provide more than clean water. It will provide freedom from searching out and paying a $1 a gallon for water in the Bahamas. This high ticket item can dramatically expand your cruising range if you so desire. If you know that you will always have water then you have peace of mind. Over the years, Wendy and I would purposefully search for the most remote anchorages that we could find. Well stocked up on food and with enough power to run the water maker, we routinely ensconced ourselves in anchorages so barren of rum shops and pizzerias that they wouldn't warrant a single word in a cruising guide.

The magic of the water maker does have its costs. If the sticker price doesn't make you weak in the knees, then your next question is 'how will I feed this power hungry consumer in a 12 volt environment?' Quest was well prepared to meet these power demands. I had equipped her with two oversized solar panels which were bolted securely to the aluminum hardtop. Our second source of renewable energy was the wind generator. And as a final backup a high output alternator was installed on the diesel engine. All of these 12 volt power sources fed a large bank of AGM batteries.

Even if you can afford a water maker and keep it powered without the cabin lights going dim there is yet the greatest problem to overcome. Where can I permanently install this new piece of bulky equipment on a sailboat that is filled to capacity? The manufacturers of water makers have a solution for installations in confined spaces. They remove the components from the enclosure in which the units are normally assembled and sell the components separately. This gave me the freedom to place a pump here, the membrane there, and filters in an easily accessible area. In one short week the water maker was bolted in and ready for testing.

If any petrochemical is present in the intake water of a water maker it can have disastrous effects on the membrane. It was highly possible that petrochemicals were present in the water at Old Port Cove, especially with a very active fuel dock operated by distracted eighteen year olds only three hundred feet away. We would take Quest out in the clean waters of the Gulf Stream and give the water maker a good run.

Although forcing high pressure salt water through a very fine membrane and extracting fresh water isn't alchemy, that doesn't mean it isn't magic. Wendy and I were both eager to see this new marvel perform in its native environment, the open ocean. The wind had freshened a bit from the north the day before the trial. A north wind tends to push up against the Gulf Stream that is coursing north at about five knots. This has the effect of creating a very bumpy confused sea. The threat of foul conditions was not a strong enough deterrent to delay the test.

We passed through the cut at the Palm Beach inlet. Our first warning of the conditions at sea was the jagged saw tooth waves that stretched across the horizon. This would not be a good day for a trip to the Bahamas. I put up the main and the yankee and we set out on a course south by south east. Within a mile of the coast we were starting to get pounded.

"We better get this done soon" I said to Wendy. "I'm getting a little light headed."

I went below and started up the water maker and returned to the cockpit. Thirty seconds later the alarm on the water maker sounded. I rebooted the water maker and tried again. As before the alarm sounded thirty seconds into the cycle. I went below for the second time with the manual under my arm. Code 33 F was flashing on the display of the controller. I searched through the manual oblivious that we were pounding through eight foot confused seas. My enemy was about to strike. Code 33 F, there was a priming problem at the main pump. At this point the words in the manual were beginning to swim around the page. I persisted in my trouble shooting until it was too late. I was getting very sick and getting worse every moment. I dragged myself into the cockpit and started the Yanmar.

"I'm dropping the main. Bring her into the wind." I loosed the main halyard and dropped the main into the lazy jacks and retired to the cockpit. "Furl the yankee and bring her home."

Those were my last words before I flopped over like a rag doll and passed out. Quest and I were now depending on Wendy's skills to get us safely back to Lake Worth. I can't remember anything after dropping the main except a montage of exceptionally evocative dreams.

"Wake up David, wake up!"

I felt Wendy's hands gently shaking my shoulders.

"Are we in Nepal? I had a dream that we were in that guesthouse in Katmandu."

"We're in Lake Worth. I can't dock Quest. You have to pull yourself out of it."

Zero G

"Forget docking right now. Head for the anchorage."

I dragged myself up on deck and pulled the release pin on the anchor and heard it plunk into the water. I lay down, curled up around the windlass and went back to Nepal.

When I returned from dream land several hours later I thought that I was in my bunk. I got up for a drink of water and nearly fell over the lifeline into Lake Worth. All I could remember from the morning's fun was a vague recollection of a morning sail.

The cause and effect relationship between motion and the onset of mal de mar is not completely known. This is evidenced by the fact that if you ask ten experts for an elaboration on the subject you are likely to get ten different answers. Equally surprising is that the symptoms of mal de mar vary greatly among its sufferers. The only constant that I have seen applied to mal de mar is that it is often placed on a one to ten scale, with zero reserved to the real men that never get sick on a boat under any conditions. A 'one' on the scale might represent mild conditions, a bit of dizziness and mild sweating. A 'ten' is a major event of discomfort on a biblical scale. What the raters of mal de mar are unaware of is that there is a reserve level on the scale that isn't commonly known. I can personally attest to the undeniable fact that the scale actually 'goes to eleven'.

Call it what you will and rate it as you please. It didn't alter the big problem that I faced. I thought that it would be imprudent of me to take Quest out on the ocean if there was any possibility of passing out for undetermined lengths of time. Many sufferers find relief with the scopolamine patch. The inherent flaw with the patch is that the delivery method is much too slow. It can take four to eight hours to be effective and you never know if you have an appropriate amount of scopolamine in your blood for current conditions. There had to be a better way to save our adventure.

I was at the PC trying my best to understand sea sickness. I was getting no where. I stepped out on the dock to stretch and greet our neighbor who was walking up the dock. Rick was a very congenial sort, highly motivated to share last night's offering of the Discovery Channel.

"Did you see the Discovery show last night? They did a piece on the Vomit Comet. You know what the Vomit Comet is?"

"No."

With great elaboration he described the NASA zero gravity simulator. It was an interesting enough subject in its own right that NASA could simulate zero gravity. It was much more interesting to me that every person that rode the Vomit Comet got seasick. If they could make somebody vomit on cue, then it was logical that NASA would have invested thought into the latest in vomit suppression.

After Rick's elaboration of the previous night's show I returned to the salon with a completely new angle on my problem. In the matter of one hour on the internet and one phone call I had all the information that I needed to make my life a little more predictable. One of the basic protocols for Vomit Comet riders at the time was an oral dose of Scopace accompanied by an oral dose of pseudo ephedrine. Scopace is scopolamine in pill form. The pseudo ephedrine is a form of amphetamine. The moderately strong depressant side effects of Scopace are countered effectively with a dose of speed. I phoned my family doctor and booked an appointment for the next day. Doctor Disco Daundia from Dubai respected the time honored traditions of South Florida. He had never found a drug he wouldn't prescribe, until now.

The next morning fresh on a mission I sat in the examining room. We briefly exchanged greetings before getting down to business.

"I need a couple of prescriptions today" I said.

"Well, what is it?"

"I need fifty Scopace."

"Sure, what's a Scopace?" he asked. I unfolded a copy of the manufacturer's brochure and handed it to him.

"OK, can you give me some idea why you think you need Scopace?"

"I'm attempting to tame the demon mal de mar."

"OK, sounds reasonable, you know that this is Scopolamine?"

"Yes doctor I know that." He wrote out the prescription. "While you're writing out prescriptions I need a second med."

"What would that be?"

"I need fifty pseudo ephedrine."

On hearing pseudo ephedrine he coughed once and spit out his breath mint. The non lethal projectile flew across the room and came to rest under the examining table.

"You've got my full attention. What are we planning to do with this pseudo ephedrine?"

"It is the second ingredient of the drug cocktail that NASA doctors administer on the Vomit Comet."

"Just take the Scopace with a caffeinated beverage."

"You can't prescribe pseudo ephedrine?" I asked.

"I won't prescribe pseudo ephedrine. Look, you must have been living in a cave for the last ten years. Pseudo ephedrine is the main ingredient in methamphetamine. You've seen the billboards on the freeway. PROBLEM WITH METH? Call 1-800… If I wrote you a prescription for pseudo ephedrine the DEA would be camped out in my waiting room within 48 hours."

His argument was most compelling. With his advice at the ready and prescription in hand I made my way to the pharmacy.

"What is Scopace? I've never heard of it and I certainly haven't dispensed it." After a brief explanation, the pharmacist took a moment and found it in a catalog. "I can have it for you by tomorrow afternoon."

I now had the magic formula, Scopace and Mountain Dew. I was armored. We set out for the second time to test the water maker but more importantly to see if the remedy would work. The problem with the water maker turned out not to be a problem at all. The vendor knew exactly what was causing the fault. The water maker was taking in air in the heavy sea and the pump was losing prime. The intake for the pump was on the port side half way up the chine. On the first test sail we were heeled hard to starboard and the intake was coming out of the water.

The day had arrived for the next test of the water maker and Scopace. The weather was horrible. It was the perfect day. The storm that blew in the week before was still with us. The seas were up and the wind was blowing twenty knots from the north-west. Testing the water maker while within the protection of the jetties would give it a fighting chance to keep the intake below the waterline. I went below and started up the system. In three minutes a stream of fresh water was issuing from the test valve. It was absolutely wonderful. I brought a glass of water to the cockpit.

"Try this" I said to Wendy. She hesitantly took a sip then a gulp.

"It's real water" she exclaimed.

Delighted by the magic of turning raw sea water into fresh water, we commenced jumping about the cockpit like lunatics drunk on water. We were approaching the last buoy at the entrance and as before that nasty looking saw tooth wave stretched across the horizon. A momentary fear gripped me, no faith in yourself? I knew that if I backed away with my tail between my legs then I likely wouldn't get a second chance. Staring down my fear I opened the Scopace bottle and popped a Scopace in my mouth. Grinding it to a horribly bitter paste in my mouth I washed it down with a Mountain Dew.

I raised the main and unfurled the yankee and set out on a course SSE. The first mile was a warm up. A mile and a half out the bow was getting battered. We were getting tossed about in the confused seas when the initial symptoms of mal de mar came on, the finger numbness and fatigue. I was too busy trying to keep the boat under control to be overly concerned with my comfort. We tried a couple of course changes trying to get into a better rhythm. There was no chance of that today. Big square waves were coming at us from all directions. But despite the uncomfortable churn my symptoms didn't get any worse. They actually faded into the background.

With the tests complete and a considerably successful day behind us, I concluded that the Scopace had a remarkable effect on controlling mal de mar in a very short time frame. We headed straight for the entrance buoys and calm waters behind the jetties. The entire time we were out in the heavy sea it was necessary to keep the companion way doors closed tight to keep out the weather. As we came into the channel I started to go below to open some hatches. When I opened the doors of the companion way and looked into the salon it was a scene of carnage. Heaps of books lay strewn about the cabin. Two locker doors had opened in the galley. In the last throes of an animated choreography, several boxes of spaghetti, plates and a variety of canned goods rolled leisurely about the sole. Spread over the entire mess was a slippery sweet sticky sheen from a shattered rum bottle. I called Wendy to the companion way door.

"Hey, this is what my brain would look like if I wasn't on drugs!"

The disarray of the cabin clearly demonstrated a trend that had to be corrected. After six months in Old

Zero G

Port Cove we had become ensconced as bona fide boat condo owners. We had become too comfortable in our leisure. Where we were about to go, fresh bagels and cream cheese couldn't follow. The hurricane season would be over in a couple of months. It was now time to meld all the pieces of our boating knowledge into a whole if we were about to tempt the fates.

We had systematically reshaped our lifestyles from land crawlers to sailors in a few short years. Even though we found the lifestyle at Old Port Cove an enjoyable alternative to reality, we were ready with anticipation to begin our adventure. Bad weather be damned, I had Scopace!

Thirteen

Dit Dot Ditty

It was October. The hurricane season was winding down for another year. We were readying boat and crew for leaving the abject poverty of our cushy digs at Old Putz Cove in North Palm Beach Florida. Under normal circumstances Wendy and I did not seek out the communion of the very well-to-do east coast borough dwellers.

Our brief one year stay at OPC favored us with a lifetime of humorous memories gleaned from the observations of a populace far older and more unforgiving than the ancient concrete docks to which we were moored. During our one year stay on our floating condo at OPC we observed with great curiosity the migratory changes that begin the day after Thanksgiving. This is the precise date that is so deeply and instinctually engrained in the snowy white fowl of the North. With the precision of the sun and stars the shiny luxury vehicles are off loaded from the trucks after their long journey from Newark. The city puts on overtime crews to systematically remove the accumulation of eight months of dust. The police department begrudgingly places their Monopoly and

Parcheesi boards in the cupboard for another year. They change the oil in the squad cars and depart out as a well trained team to clean the town of all undesirables not wearing coordinated outerwear. The lawn care specialists, carpet cleaners, and painters blend into the background to make room for an instant billion dollar traffic jam. As the population increases so does the snarl of traffic. As one would expect, this snarl could be heard in every business establishment in North Palm. From the grocery store to the mall, the all too blunt expostulating crowd of visitors didn't seem at all capable of finding anything to their liking. This seasonal cultural change served to keep the migratory masses soothed.

Except for brief and infrequent forays into the mean streets of North Palm we stayed sequestered behind the locked and guarded gates of Old Putz Cove. The original purpose of our stay at OPC was coming to a conclusion. In simplest terms we would slip out of Lake Worth Inlet and sail south for the Caribbean with no plans to return. Theoretically we were totally prepared. I had just completed the full overhaul of Quest, our 1986 Bayfield 36. This labour of love took me the best part of two years. Among our collection of high tech toys was a brand new full frequency Icom brand Single Side Band. It was a very stout digital SSB transceiver that at the time of installation only lacked the essential option, a licensed operator. Feeling that responsibility firmly resting on my shoulders I set out to acquire my Amateur Radio operator's license. I only had a month or so to learn and pass the technician license and then sit for the general license. The general license would give me full use of the long distance voice frequencies.

Learning Morse code is a challenge. The first approach of most self taught Morse code inductees is to view the process of coding like learning another language relying heavily on memorization. Although there is certainly a great deal of memorizing it is only the first step. In learning a new language one must embrace a lexicon, a linguistic methodology, and attempt to integrate the two in such a way that communication within that system is rendered useful. Morse code is not a language even though I tried to trick myself into thinking so. The beginning of training in Morse code is to learn the symbolic equivalent of every letter, number, and common punctuation. The letter A is coded: dit dash; an N is coded dash dit. There are in all about forty letters, numbers and punctuation that have to be learned and retained. To simply learn and remember the corresponding code for the alphabet and numbers is a bit of a challenge but it is only the first baby step in learning to be proficient in sending and receiving code.

Morse code is definitely not a language, no more than alphabet soup is a language. A more appropriate description is that Morse code is machine language. It bears a very strong resemblance to its offspring, binary computer code. Just as Morse code could not exist without coding all letters in to dits and dashes, the computer would not exist without the binary coding of ones and zeroes.

If there are any similarities between Morse code and language it is only in their respective abilities to communicate an idea. The ability of a language to transmit an idea or concept is not wholly dependent on the accurate rendering of the words in a phrase. Nor is it dependent on accurate spelling or punctuation. The words in a sentence could be spelled wrong or a spoken phrase could be pronounced inaccurately and still be understood perfectly well. To some extent a communicated phrase or even a word can be looked upon as a whole which represents a specific idea.

The application of Morse code is in stark contrast to language. If each letter, number and punctuation is represented by a series of dits and dashes these forty symbols are set in a purely logical framework. Then unlike language, which is inherently illogical, there is absolutely no room for error when the sender and receiver of Morse code attempt to communicate. All languages generously permit mistakes. Morse code is cold and completely unforgiving. With Morse code you either recognize the letters and symbols or you don't. Individuals who are overly dependent on the very accommodating nature of our written and spoken language will find the learning of Morse code particularly difficult. To my misfortune I was one of those doomed individuals.

Most forms of communication can be thought of as two discreet activities. Half of communication is sending an idea. The other side is receiving. Language, whether it is Fiji, Dutch or English, is first spoken; the listener interprets and replies. This commonplace chain of events is carried out unconsciously and without much fanfare in normal conversation.

When one attempts to learn international Morse code the contrast between sending and receiving is very dramatic. Sending and receiving take on two distinct forms. In comparison coding a word into dits and dashes relies heavily on a logical thought process. Relative to decoding it is very easy. Everyone knows from childhood that the international distress signal is SOS. SOS expressed in Morse code is (dit,dit,dit...dash,dash,dash...dit,dit,dit). This is probably the simplest of all coded messages. As long as the listener can distinguish the fundamental dit and dash and count to three the SOS can be easily translated. In the case of an SOS broadcast in Morse code the sender normally broadcasts a constant series of SOS's. Even a person who knows nothing about Morse code could send a distress signal. It isn't critical to the message to even know what code sequence represents an S or what represents an O. It is enough that an operator sends a series of three dits followed by three dashes even though it will be read by the receiver as SOSOSOSO. This repeated series of letters which doesn't represent a technically accurate SOS distress call will be read and interpreted by even a novice receiver as a meaningful message.

The skill one must acquire to send Morse code is in stark contrast to the ability to receive. To send a message the beginner has the simple and straight forward task of bringing to mind the Morse code equivalent of the letter and tapping the code out with a finger. The usual method at the very beginning of self instruction is to tap out messages on a table top with an index finger and thumb, A.... dit dash, B.....dash dit dit dit until all the letters and symbols can be remembered. At this point there is little need for accuracy. The exercise is designed not so much to train for exactitude but to drive the average person completely insane. This state of self inflicted madness provides ample insulation from the pain of turning a perfectly normal well operating illogical mind to a mind obsessed and operating on the pure logic of a digital language.

I personally did not sink into the abyss of induced insanity as easy as most. I desperately held on to my irrationality as long as I possibly could. I finally succumbed one evening while watching a movie in the saloon of Quest. We had rented the Arnold Schwarzenegger movie 'Terminator'. For those readers not acquainted with the movie, there is a recurring low frequency monotone theme that sounds something like: 'da dit. da… da'. Without my full volition my index finger began tapping out the same sequence for the letters 'Y'…Dash dit dash dash.

If this wasn't sufficient to propel me head first down the rabbit hole of insanity, Wendy at that time was just starting a batch of pop corn in the galley. While I watched the intro of 'Terminator' and at the same time mechanically tapped out 'Y's' on the table top, the popcorn started to pop. My Morse code induced trance quickly expanded to a mind numbing harmony of 'pop pop….pop, pop, pop…pop', 'da dit. da… da'. Without my full knowledge I had become entranced by the code. As the movie played on and the pop corn continued to pop I sat poised at my station decoding the subtle messages transmitted by Hollywood and Orville Redenbacher. The popcorn soliloquy finally ended and the culprits consumed. The movie ended, good triumphed. But I was left dangling

147

with one foot in the normal world of the average human and the other foot in the secret and mysterious world of Morse code.

My movie and popcorn indoctrination into the World of Morse was just a beginning. Once the mind has hold of such an object of focus there is no halting its progress until an adequate conclusion is reached. After the movie I lay in my bunk. A 25 knot wind blew through the harbor, the lanyards rhythmically slapped against my neighbors masts. The sound of boats squeaking against fenders, even the dripping of my galley sink spoke in Morse code. A great deal of this naturally induced code was unintelligible. The more interesting coded messages which could be derived from the bumps, dings, squeaks and drips happened in that twilight state just before deep sleep. With the help of a willing mind about to enter dreamland I was able to decode elaborate messages on subjects upon which I would not wish to elaborate.

The next morning greeted a person subjected to a night of phantom messages. With my mind somewhat clearer I returned to a state in which I could draw definite conclusions regarding the previous night's coded messages. The absolute and definite conclusion was that I couldn't have been hearing messages in the rigging. The fact that I couldn't read Morse code with any degree of accuracy was the smoking gun. In the previous two weeks I had been diligent in learning to send code. I had downloaded a software program that gave me the ability to send and receive code. Like most novices I focused exclusively on sending, sending being a rather simple and low skill when compared to receiving. The code requirements to procure an amateur radio operating license only included receiving. The logic is that if one can receive then one can send.

The test was two weeks away and I was determined to take and pass the test at any cost. My receiving skills were so bad at that point that I would get muddled up on just a couple of words, let alone receiving a fifty word message. I needed a better way to learn to receive. The answer to my problem was shipped that day from a vendor of Morse code training devices. It was a small slim device about the size of a hand held calculator with a pair of ear phones attached and an LCD display. All that the trainee needed to do was turn it on, set the send speed and press go. The device generated random Morse code messages which would appear on the screen after a message was sent. I now could listen to 500 messages repeated randomly, when and for as long as I wished.

In the next four days the earphones rested securely on my ears. I read, worked on the repairs on Quest, cooked, ate and slept with the code generator beeping out 35 words a minute in Morse code. The only change in this pattern occurred during the three minute interlude that was infrequently needed to change the batteries. My proficiency at decoding developed painfully slow at first. Then within four days I had not only gotten a moderate grasp of Morse code but I had also memorized every one of the random messages that the device could generate. By the sixth day I could guess with relative certainty what message would randomly be generated next. If you know what code is about to be generated then the tool becomes completely ineffectual. I needed more messages. I downloaded another 500 messages from the vendor's Internet site. When I started the next batch of messages I was surprised to find that my skills had been significantly weakened by repetition of the first batch of memorized messages. I pressed on and overindulged in the next 500 messages.

I never did reach a point with Morse code where I had developed any degree of skill or acceptable proficiency. I highly suspected that my ability to retain my freshly learned skills would evaporate shortly after I had taken the test on the next Saturday morning. For that reason alone I knew that if I stopped for even one day my chances of passing would be slim. Saturday arrived.

The test was scheduled for 10 AM in one of the meeting rooms at the VA hospital in Riviera Beach, Florida. I arrived at 8:00 and found the room locked where the test was to be held. My plan was to put in a couple more hours decoding before the test.

I wandered the halls of the hospital until I came across the chapel. I sat in a back pew in the dark, did a quick battery change and went back to work. It would add considerable complexity and sparkle to the story if I could report a divine intervention; the hand of God gently resting on my head followed by a brief but distinctive message sent from the ethereal plain in Morse code assuring me that 'every thing was going to be alright… everything's going to be all right' maybe with a bit of Bob Marley playing in the distant background. But this was a non-denominational chapel where territorial disputes and divine infighting do not encourage the more commonplace spontaneous miracle. What did happen was that one of the Morse code examiners read the note that I had left on the examination room door, came into the chapel, gave me a firm squeeze on my shoulder and told me that I had about five minutes to get my butt in a seat in the examination room.

There was only a small turnout for the General operators test. The group included me and three rather over confident males in their early twenties. From the good hearted banter among the three gents I ascertained that they all had studied the code together and judging from their Morse code inspired jokes they were quite proficient at receiving.

The four of us sat and we were first handed the written portion of the General license test. The written test is a series of multiple choice questions designed to test understanding of electronics and the rules regarding the use of a Ham radio. After the allotted time the tests were graded. We all passed with good grades.

We were now shepherded into a room with a cassette player on a table attached to speakers. We were issued a pair of number two pencils and a sheet of paper. We would listen and decode for about five minutes, writing the message on the paper. Then there would be a 25 word fill-in-the-blank test based on the received code. The recording began. I fought for every letter. I was decoding a little less than seventy-five percent of the letters. The recording stopped and we were handed the written test. With my patchy decoding and a bit of logic I was able to get a passing grade. My fellow students didn't fare as well. Of the three not one of them got even one letter of the five minute message. Perhaps they were consoled by the soothing remark: "Don't feel bad boys. Nobody passes on their first try." I was congratulated and handed my temporary license. I was now a binary coding machine:

KG4 WQK.   "-.- --. ...- .-- --.- -.-"

Fourteen

Florida Farewell

Our heroes now lie at anchor two hundred feet from Lake Worth Inlet poised on America's doorstep. Half the world was trying to get into America with Wendy and I trying to get out. If one is going to leave the 'land of the free and the home of the brave' then going off sailing into the unknown without a firm plan and for an undetermined length of time offered us a fresh and exciting approach. While our enthusiasm would help us tremendously in reaching these undetermined goals, our boating skills lacked refinement. We were floating condo owners. During our ownership of Quest we had been out sailing no more than a dozen times. On each occasion the primary reason for leaving the dock was of a purely practical nature. We sailed expressly to test and tune the many systems that I had installed during Quest's retrofit. We didn't sail for the sheer pleasure of being on the water. We sailed purposely. Quest was our portable home.

I would be the first to admit that leaving the protection of Florida and sailing into the North Atlantic with practically no experience could be seen by some as a risky affair. As a matter of fact I was usually quick to agree with our more salty brethren when they expressed their compelling arguments on the need for advanced seamanship. The attempts of our educators to moderate our goals and have us see reason had no effect on our sailing plans despite their ominous tone. But we became convinced that if we were leaving ourselves open to disaster then our only defense was to rely on our meager assets among which were the undeniable sea worthiness of Quest, a good foundation in theoretical seamanship, and good trip planning. We did have the most intangible assets of all. We were confident and Wendy and I were compatible.

The sea can certainly be a dangerous place and at the same time a wondrous place. It is a place that rewards the strong and the resourceful. It will brutally punish the weak. For a cruising couple that embarks on an extended voyage the greatest danger is not the stress and wear from these ever present forces of nature. It is not even their ability to keep a cool head in a life threatening emergency. Cruising couples face the possible horrors of incompatibility. Inhabiting a twelve foot by thirty foot cabin with someone that you have grown to despise is definitely a horror.

The far majority of couples that try their hand at ocean cruising are in their latter years. They have a good cruising kitty. For the most part, their boats are safe and comfortable. They have a lifetime of sailing skills. For half of these adventurers the dream dies within the first year. Remove this upper middle class gentry from the normal routine of two strangers with separate lives meeting briefly to exchange pleasantries in a 3000 square foot house and place them side by side day in, day out with no escape and their compatibility is tested. It is far beyond my ability to understand compatibility. But if you and your spouse can live on a boat for one year without giving up on the relationship, you have something special. Wendy and I have a compatible relationship that defies logic. On most days we are argumentative, bull-headed, loud and highly demonstrative. This is before lunch and just a warm-up for the afternoon. To the consternation of most innocent bystanders our storms arise and blow over like quick squalls with perfect weather to follow. More importantly, before and after the storms, we always remain each others unqualified best friend.

Just as compatibility on a cruising boat is crucial, the ability to keep an open sailing schedule is vital to good trip planning. Most seasoned cruisers worst stories of woe at sea usually began with a theme: 'Had to be there then'. All too often a couple would throw themselves into horrible weather conditions simply to satisfy a schedule. 'We have to be there by the 21st to pick up my sister'… 'The reason we got in that big storm was because we had to meet Fred in the Abacos on the 10th'. These stories were the norm. We were constantly meeting couples who had sailed through heavy weather just to satisfy the transient need to be somewhere else. In almost all cases the couples were quick to admit their lack of foresight. But they would go out and take a pounding a week later just to be on time. The financially independent cruiser who worked a lifetime had held doggedly to rigid schedules and goals. When this over achiever chooses the cruising life they don't change the habits of a lifetime. Many cruisers, especially the part time winter cruisers are, always, in a hurry, to go everywhere. Judging by popular opinion and the consistent reproach of our peers, our habit of waiting for a weather window left us in the minority.

To make the most of weather and rarely be surprised by bad conditions requires a method of predicting weather that is accurate and portable. A cruising boat is in many ways an autonomous entity. There is no weather channel at sea. In the majority of our cruising grounds there wasn't anything even resembling Coast Guard broadcast weather reports on the VHF. Our most common form of weather predicting was analyzing the daily weather Fax broadcast by the U.S. Coast Guard over the Single Side Band Radio. The process is straight forward. The U.S. Coast Guard transmitter in southern Louisiana transmits a fax signal on a daily schedule. The mariner receives the signal. This voice frequency signal is demodulated with a modem then downloaded into a software program on a PC. The program then paints relatively slow but accurate data onto the screen of the PC in the form of a weather chart which is then saved and interpreted. With a bit of study, a SSB, and a computer anybody can learn to be a weather expert.

We waited at anchor for just over a week before we got our weather window to cross the strait. The distance between Riviera Beach and West End is only 65 miles. It wasn't the distance that delayed our crossing for a week. It wasn't the fifteen knot wind from the north or the five knot current in the Gulf Stream. It was the combination of these two forces that can turn the Gulf Stream into an impenetrable wall for a small boat. We were waiting at anchor for just such an event to pass. Two weeks prior to our crossing, the leading edge of a stationary weather system over Georgia brought fifteen to twenty knots of wind against the flow of the Stream. This is a very normal condition in South Florida in autumn. When this strong north wind blows in opposition to a strong current it causes the waves to pile up into a disorganized mess of confused square topped waves. Even a boater on a schedule would have reservations about venturing into the strait under such conditions. The rest usually turn back. If they don't they may even live to tell the big adventure story.

While the strait raged a mile from our anchorage Wendy and I patiently practiced the art of waiting for weather. When the wind from the north veers south, the current and wind work in tandem. When the wind blows with the Stream at fifteen knots, the sea conditions will be very mild and comfortable. The day before our departure the wind was fifteen knots north by northwest with a long and leisurely ocean swell from the south.

Comparing the two common types of pleasure craft which routinely cross to the Bahamas, power boats have many advantages. A power boat capable of thirty knots can be in the Bahamas before lunch. They travel a straight rhumb line bouncing along wave tops with their shallow v-hull not presenting any great broadside to the current. In contrast a sailboat like Quest has a six foot full keel and moves at an average speed of five knots. The forceful current of the Gulf Stream striking the long profile of our keel would have to be considered when we planned our trip. Even though our destination was practically due east, we needed to factor the strong northerly effect of the stream and actually sail south at the beginning of the voyage so that when we exited the stream about half way across the strait we wouldn't be pushed too far to the north. This maneuver would add at least thirty degrees of southing to the initial course direction. Sailing this prescribed parabolic course would add about ten miles to the trip. So instead of a sixty-five mile sail it would actually be a seventy-five mile sail with no consideration for distance lost to tacking.

The seventy-five mile trip at 4.5 knots would theoretically take around sixteen hours. It is most desirable to arrive in a new destination during daylight hours. The sun would set on the following day at approximately 6 PM. The weather and the sailing conditions in the strait are quite fickle. We felt very fortunate to get a weather window so quickly. It was going to be a long day beginning with a 2:30 AM departure the following morning.

Lake Worth Inlet is a dredged cut through a barrier island. The cut is almost a half mile long, a quarter of a mile wide and 35 feet deep. The millions of tons of sand that were dredged from the channel were dumped in a very large spoils pile that is called Peanut Island. Peanut Island is home to one of the remaining relics of the cold war and a reminder of the threat of nuclear destruction. In the 1960's during the buildup to the Cuban missile crisis the Navy Seabees at the request of President Kennedy built in just nine days a modest nuclear fall out shelter on Peanut Island. The shelter is a five minute helicopter ride from the

Kennedy compound in Palm Beach. For a few dollars anyone can take a fifteen minute ride into a piece of terrifying history. But the Lake Worth inlet was dredged many years before the military industrial complex beat the drum in support of their grandiose business model.

The modest engineering feat of dredging the Lake Worth Inlet was not undertaken to accommodate pleasure craft. It was dredged and maintained to its current dimensions by the Federal government to serve the commercial port of Riviera Beach.

There were two general categories of ships which sailed past our cockpit the night before we left for the Caribbean. The most common was the large and quiet cargo container ships. The cargo ships were very well mannered. They would pass mostly unnoticed if it wasn't for their substantial bow wave that jostled us around in the anchorage.

The second category of ship was locally referred to as the 'party boat'. It looked like a gaily painted three hundred foot long floating metal box. The singular purpose of the party boat was to board five percent more tourists than their licenses allowed, wallow out to sea, get the patrons into a pleasantly inebriated state, and then relieve them of as many dollars as possible at the gaming tables.

I believe the greatest benefit of the party boats was not as an instrument of higher social good but rather as a source of amusement to the fishermen watching the antics pass by from their lawn chairs on the jetty. The party boat even had it's own theme music, 'Who let the dogs out", blasting from manhole sized speakers at 120 decibels. "Who let the dogs out" was originally written and produced for the Trinidad and Tobago Carnival, which is a nation-size version of the Riviera Beach party boat. I use the term 'written' very loosely since "who let the dogs out" was the only intelligible line in the entire song. But a party boat wouldn't be a party without guest participation. Whenever the refrain of the song blasted "who let the dogs out" a squad of colorfully dressed cruise directors cued the patrons to scream "WOOF WOOF". This hundred plus chorus had an auditory range of about two miles. So there we were, anchored next to the channel, trying to get a few hours sleep before our big adventure with the primal screams of "WOOF WOOF" drumming on the hull.

In the early hour of 2:30 AM we were dressed, anchor up, and a pot of breakfast porridge secured between the stove-top fiddles. We threaded Quest out the channel on a dark moonless night. When we cleared the final buoy, we came into the wind and raised the main and both headsails. We turned off the auxiliary and set the autopilot for an intercept course with the Gulf Stream. We were flying headlong into the darkness at a dizzying six knots.

The topic of conversation as we watched the lights twinkle in the condos in Palm Beach and ate our breakfast was how we would react to being out of the sight of land for the first time in our lives. Would it be frightening when land disappeared and we were alone in the big sea? We didn't have to wait long for an answer. The shoreline slowly disappeared. Then the brightly lighted high rises disappeared one floor at a time until the top floors of the buildings winked out for good. We sailed into the night for several hours until the false dawn cast dark violet hues on the east horizon. The cloudless dawn was magnificent with the first rays of light catching every ripple. After experiencing the dark of night, and then dawn on a cloudless sky, the light reflecting off the ocean looked as though the waves were being set on fire. The sunrise also brought our first true experience of being alone at sea. To our surprise we found the solitude was not frightening. We didn't feel any desperate need to turn around and go back. It wasn't bravery that sent us forth. It was the fear of having to live in South Florida any longer.

We sailed on a solid broad reach with Quest's bow plunging head long into the full velocity of the Gulf Stream which slowed our progress by a full two knots. When we finally reached the bottom of the parabola, we were in position to make our tack and set the sails for our arrival in West End, Grand Bahama Island. As we turned northerly and began our run, the force of the stream added two knots to our speed. Our hull speed was about five knots but our speed over ground was about seven knots. With momentum like this we would be in West End well before we had planned.

Around noon we noticed that the wind was shifting a bit to the east. Then the wind slowly began to lay down and finally became very erratic. Quest slowed to a crawl, and if we were to make the next twenty miles before dark we had to motor. The party was over for today. We would be smelling diesel fumes for the next several hours. I started the auxiliary, lowered the sails and brought the diesel up to the required rpm that would ensure our 6 PM arrival.

About one hour into our motoring I was snoozing in the cockpit when two engine alarms abruptly woke me from a fleeting dream. The alternator annunciator and the engine temperature sensor were buzzing and blinking. I switched off the Yanmar.

"Try to keep the boat into the swell as much as possible" I said to Wendy as I tore off the engine cover.

I searched for the problem. The alternator belt was torn to shreds and lay in the engine sump. I whipped the tattered belt into the cockpit and yelled "Watch out! BLACK SNAKE!" My well-rehearsed snake joke lacked a sense of spontaneity forty miles out at sea.

"Do you know where a fresh belt is?" Wendy asked sternly.

"Not exactly" I said.

"If you promise never to use that raggedy old snake gag, I'll tell you."

"I agree."

"They're under the charts in the rear berth."

I located and quickly installed the new belt.

"Fire up the engine" I said.

We were off in record time. The small inconvenience of replacing the belt added about twenty minutes to our sailing time. I throttled the diesel up to about 2200 rpm and kept my fingers crossed and hoped that another belt wouldn't break. The sun was approaching the horizon and the GPS put us five miles from our destination. We couldn't see any signs of land. Was our GPS wrong? Not so, it was just one of the three thousand flat Bahama Islands. West End came in sight just as the

Florida Farewell

navigational lights blinked on at Old Bahama Bay Marina
on Grand Bahama Island.

Fifteen

Grand Bahama Island

Our voyage from Riviera Beach, Florida to West End on Grand Bahama Island was the successful start of our two thousand mile journey to Trinidad. Every experience that day was exciting and challenging for Quest's eager rookie crew. It was the first time we had sailed out of US waters. It was our first time in the open ocean. It was even the first time that we had sailed at night. In the upcoming months with a few hundred miles under the keel these modest beginnings would seem routine.

The first requirement in entering the Bahamas or any country's territorial waters is to pay a visit to and be greeted by Customs and Immigration. The Bahamian government does everything in their power to make this experience friendly and streamlined. More importantly they have structured the arrival fees charged to the recreational boater like a well designed foreign aid program. Arriving at Customs the boater is brought before the chief financial inquisitor who with the skill of a bond trader assays your financial worth. This estimate determines your personally tailored package of fees, bribes and extortion. There is the entry fee, the cruising fee, the fishing fee, pet fee, and the exit fee. Some boaters have claimed that they were nickeled and dimed at Customs. Our entrance fee was an even three hundred dollars, no change. Bahama entry fees comprised half of all the fees that we would pay in our five years in the Caribbean.

If there is a bit of sticker shock associated with the entry fees, it only serves to guide the visitor into a full appreciation of the Bahamian style of governance. The Bahamian Government has a successful history of exploiting their strategic and isolated position one hundred miles from the US coast. Lacking resources, or the inclination to produce any product, they have styled their economy to resemble a happy smiling version of Black Beard the pirate. Without even enough potable water in the country to grow a tomato plant they have managed with both the help and consternation of the international community to build a banking system for the discriminating shopper. But laundering money can't build a robust economy from sand. Selling small private islands to fugitives and providing convenient transshipment points for the South American recreational drug trade fills out their portfolio to the point that they can easily buy the best tomatoes from Holland.

Wendy and I did not sail to the Bahama Islands to study racketeering or to hob knob with prominent modern day buccaneers. Our goal was to enjoy our passage from West End on Grand Bahama and then sail through the entire Bahama chain. We anticipated several months of smooth sailing before arriving in the northern Turks. We were particularly looking forward to indulging our desire for solitude in the many sparsely populated anchorages along our route. Before we could hide out on deserted islands we had one short detour. The plan was to dock at a marina about half way down Grand Bahama Island for the evening and leave at 2 AM the next morning for Great Stirrup Island. The marina would put us within walking distance of a sight seeing trip and fresh grocery run to Freeport. Because of its close proximity to Florida the Grand Bahama Island marinas can get busy so Wendy volunteered to call up Running Mon Marina and see if she could book a slip.

She came back and reported that "Running Mon can only guarantee a slip if we come today. He told me that he will hold the slip until five o'clock."

"Did you ask him about the depth in the channel?"

"He said that the channel isn't a problem but if our draft was six feet then we should come at high tide and stick to the right side of the entrance."

Within several hours we would have our first lesson in the dangers of believing the navigational doublespeak of the average marina manager when they describe the navigability of their facilities.

We felt pretty lucky to get dockage at Running Mon as we left Old Bahama Bay marina in West End. We would arrive about noon at Running Mon marina right on schedule for high tide. And if that wasn't lucky enough, it was a high spring tide. We were planning to leave the next morning for Great Stirrup Island. We had a very pleasant morning sail along the coast of Grand Bahama Island uneventfully reaching our way point just outside the marina entrance. I made my approach into the channel at a snails pace just to the right side of the entrance keeping one eye on the depth finder.

"I'm running out of water" I said to Wendy.

"He did tell me that the entrance was a bit shallow but the channel had plenty of water."

Just as I was about to announce that we had one inch of water the starboard aft portion of the keel struck a submerged rock ledge. Quest's stern rose and rocked to port with a low grinding sound. I opened the throttle as wide as it could go. Quest rocked several times, gouging more fiberglass from the keel and slowly bumped her way off the ledge.

The channel into Running Mon marina was a quarter of a mile long. In their brochures they had boasted about their full service boat yard on the premises. I couldn't see the marina but the boat yard was coming in view. I took up the binoculars.

"Take a look at a full service boat yard" I said to Wendy as I handed her the glasses. An old rusted derelict travel lift was poised over the lift slip. Half of its parts had been cannibalized. The doors and windows of the buildings were boarded up. Three foot scraggy weeds grew in the parking lot. Even this sign of decay couldn't have prepared us for our next visual double take. We turned the corner into the marina. The entire marina was completely empty, devoid of water craft of any size or description. Right in the middle of this ghostly scene was the marina manager smiling and waving, gesturing us to throw him our dock lines.

"So where are all the boats?" I yelled over the gunwales.

"Oh, the boats, ah… they left yesterday."

I turned my head away and whispered to Wendy "Former Miami boat dealer?"

She acknowledged with raised eyebrows.

I shook his hand and said "I think there's a little bit less than six feet of water out there."

He replied "It must be low tide."

As we walked from the dock to the office to fill out paperwork, the state of Running Mon marina unfolded like the abandoned movie set of the low budget cataclysm movie… 'Where did all the people go?' The highly touted luxury resort was also completely empty; no plump tourists eating their fifth meal of the morning, no lobster colored children charbroiling beside the pool. All signs indicated that the throngs did not depart the previous day with the phantom boaters. The chain link fence at the entrance was padlocked. As we passed the full service chandlery I noticed it too was padlocked, shelves empty apart from a modest layer of dust. The duty free shop sat locked and empty; Customs/Immigration, empty. We were escorted into the marina office where a card table occupied one corner of a bare room with three badly worn folding chairs keeping it company. A rude bookshelf of rough lumber bolted to a wall served as a repository for a modest selection of tattered cruising guides, local tourist propaganda and a VHF radio drumming out hurricane scares from Miami.

"Where's the maddening crowd?" I quipped.

"It's the off season" he said.

"The off season?... This is the off season? It's mid November!"

This disheveled, sunken eyed fugitive from the South Miami nightclub scene stood up on his hind legs, extended himself to his full five foot four inch stature and proudly announced "We're renovating the marina."

"Ten thirty… Wednesday morning. Where's the construction crew?"

"They're gone to lunch. Look, if you don't want to stay here then leave!" he announced with belligerence.

"If I could, I would."

"What are you getting at?" he said pushing his interrogatory range.

"My friend, due primarily to your dubious expert navigational advice regarding the entrance depth of the channel we are locked up in Running Mon marina as tight as the proverbial ship in a bottle. The tide won't be high enough to get out of the entrance for two weeks. Considering that this is only half a marina I expect to pay half the rate."

It turned out to be a well-placed shot over the yardarms. There was lonely written all over his unshaven face. He was ready for some company.

"OK" he said in a most congenial fashion.

Wendy handed him a credit card.

"Do you have any cash?" he asked.

"We'll work it out" I said.

We left him in the office in solitude. As we walked back to Quest I looked at Wendy and said "That went well.

Half price in the Bahamas."

When I examined the bottom of Quest, I found four nasty gouges on the aft bottom that marred an otherwise perfect bottom job. Our electronic tide charts put the next spring tide in two weeks. To be certain, we would sound the depth of the entrance at the next high tide. At 11:00 PM we dinghied to the entrance with a flashlight and a coil of string tied to a brick. We had calibrated our improvised depth sounder and placed knots at five feet and one inch increments after that. The sea was calm so the reading would be accurate. I slowly lowered the brick on the string. The brick rested on the rock bottom. I pulled the slack out of the string. Wendy shined the light on the string.

"We're not leaving tonight" she said. "I read five feet eight inches."

"Four inches shy" I sighed.

We surveyed back and forth across the entrance and we couldn't find more than five foot nine inches. We were trapped. Fortunately our stint in Running Mon Marina was not indefinite. The next chance to sail Quest above the rocks would be in two weeks at two o'clock in the morning on a particularly high spring tide.

As we turned the dinghy into the channel I spotted a ghostly figure standing on the break wall adjacent to the derelict marina office. Wendy spotted it seconds later.

"Do you see that?" she whispered over the put-put of the outboard.

"That's the ghost of Running Mon. He only appears at midnight of high tide" I said.

"Well, the ghost of Running Mon has a flashlight

and he's waving us over" she replied.

We motored up to the break wall and threw Running Mon the dinghy's line.

"You two from boat in marina?"

"We're from Quest" I said.

"What you do in channel?"

"We're night fishing" I said.

He cast the beam of the flashlight into the bottom of the dinghy.

"You fish with brick?"

"Brick fishing. You wait for a fish to come by and you drop the brick on its head."

He let out a suppressed chuckle which was followed by friendly laughter that echoed off the walls of the empty resort.

"You funny Mon captain. I Jake. I night watchman."

"Nice to meet you. She's Wendy and I'm David" I said. "We were out checking the depth of the entrance."

"Watch dat entrance. It get bit shallow for boat like yours."

"The manager told us that there is plenty of water."

"That manager never been in boat in life."

I shook his hand.

"Hey, take this brick, it's one of yours."

I handed him the brick and we pushed off.

Being stuck in Running Mon didn't delay our schedule in the least. We had no schedule. We were paying minimal dockage rates which we would turn to our advantage. It took a good deal of walking in Freeport on the first two days to determine that the padlocked environs of Running Mon Marina and our home aboard Quest held far more interest to Wendy and I than did anything else on Grand Bahama Island. But we didn't want to just idle away two weeks. We needed a boat project. I had stored two quarts of interior varnish in a rear locker. This was an opportune time to remove every bit of teak from the inside of Quest, place all the items on the dock, wet sand with 400 grit and slap on a few coats of varnish.

After breakfast Wendy piled the contents of all the drawers onto the rear berth, carried the drawers onto the dock and arranged them in a row. I removed all the doors and stretched them out lengthwise on the dock. This assortment of teak joinery occupied about thirty five feet of prime dock space. We were in the process of preparing for a day of varnishing when I first heard the faint throb of an outboard.

"Do you hear a big outboard engine?" I asked Wendy.

"It's getting really close" she replied.

Within seconds a forty foot sparkling double v-hull came blasting into the marina creating a wave that swamped the dock and our nicely prepped teak. They raced up in front of the office and made a dramatic 180 degree power turn. The boat hadn't even come close to the dock before the female passenger leaped out and threw the bow line over the cleat. While she secured the boat in great haste the man at the wheel held a cell phone tightly to his right ear and was madly gesturing in the air with his left hand.

With the boat secured the pair disappeared into the cabin. What was going on in that cabin? Were they late for a plane? Was somebody hurt? In less than three minutes a taxi ground to a halt in the gravel just outside the marina gate, stopping in a cloud of dust and honked its horn. If this was an emergency it was definitely a well planned one. Before the taxi's dust had a chance to settle, our mysterious pair flew through the companionway each struggling with overweight large canvas gym bags. They jumped to the dock, raced to the taxi and jumped in. The taxi sped away out of sight. This little bit of excitement livened up the cloistered sanctuary of Running Mon Marina. This was Act One.

During the intermission that followed, Wendy and I dried the splashed teak and prepped it for varnishing. Fifteen minutes after the taxi left, a small car eased up to the marina and parked behind the office out of sight. Two men, one black and one white in their thirties, both a lean six feet tall, well-armed and dressed in well to do club apparel strolled casually over to the docked V-hull. They boarded, forced their way into the companionway and disappeared inside. As a concerned busybody I walked to the marina office to report a possible crime in progress.

"What's going on with that boat that just raced in here?" I asked the manager.

The manger stared at the floor and very emphatically ordered me to return to my boat and don't get involved. I did as I was advised.

Wendy and I couldn't even guess where this little drama was heading. After about an hour when the adrenalin tapered off and we'd finished varnishing, the same taxi that first picked up the power boaters slid to a halt in the gravel outside the gate. Our mystery mariners exited the taxi without the two heavy gym bags. They casually strode to their boat and boarded. When they opened the companionway two pairs of hands reached out and dragged them both bodily into the cabin. For several minutes the boat rocked and shook violently at the dock while oaths and threats issued from the portholes. Our marina neighbors were then shoved through the companionway in handcuffs and thrown roughly onto the dock. They were promptly stuffed into the back of the small car that had been parked out of sight beside the office.

So far in thirteen days of cruising we had left the protected waters of the United States, successfully crossed one of the most feared stretches of water on the east coast, almost tore the bottom out of Quest, got trapped in a ghost marina, and were witnesses to the capture and arrest of a pair of international criminals. The novelty of these early experiences was soon to be over-shadowed by the next Bahamian drama.

'Time and tide wait for no man.' Our two weeks of waiting for the high spring tide was finally over. At two o'clock the next morning the tide would be high enough to float Quest over the rocks. We would be freed from our lunar sequestration in Running Mon Marina.

Sixteen

The Berries

A ghostly calm had settled over Running Mon Marina the night before we left for the Berry Islands. Even Jake the night watchman succumbed to this overpowering sense of emptiness. He sat slumbering with his chair propped up against the wall in the solitude of a warm clear Bahama night. He wore a ball cap pulled tightly over his forehead shielding his eyes from the bright moonlight. Who could blame any body for sleeping at Running Mon Marina? Just one look at the empty docks and deserted resort at midnight would be a sufficient narcotic for any insomniac.

In contrast to the nocturnal activities of Slumber Mon, Wendy and I were wide awake at midnight preparing for our 2 AM departure. The moon was full. The tide was as high as it would be in four months. After two weeks of waiting for this very high spring tide to float us over the rocks at the entrance we would now be free to continue our journey south. I turned the key in the ignition. The throb of the Yanmar echoed softly off the surrounding buildings. Our crack security force opened one eye, eased his chair forward and sprang up.

"Hey Sleepy Mon" I shouted to our able guard.

"Hey funny Mon, you go brick fishin' tonight?"

"Yeah we're going brick fishing" I said. "This time we're bringing the big brick."

Jake most ceremonially ran to our dock and untied our fore and aft lines.

"Good night for fishin" he said.

"Sweet dreams Running Mon" I whispered from the cockpit as he tossed Wendy the fore and aft line.

I spun Quest around and cleared my head for the quarter mile run down the unlighted channel. Wendy was at the bow sweeping with a spotlight. I kept one eye on the moonlit banks of the channel and one eye on the depth gauge. The rock shelf that two weeks before had scraped our hull and trapped us in Running Mon was right between the two entrance navigational lights. The navigational lights at the entrance of Running Mon served as a reminder of the importance the Bahamians place on all navigational aids. They were broken. Wendy shone the spotlight on the unlit markers. I held my breath. We cleared the rock ledge with two inches of water under the keel. We were finally free of Running Mon Marina.

Today's 67 mile jaunt was starting out very well on a beautiful starry night. A strong weather event had been stationary in the Atlantic one hundred miles north east of Grand Bahama Island. Running Mon Marina was in the lee of the storm on the southwest side of Grand Bahama Island. We sailed in a very mild breeze and calm seas for five miles until we slowly came out of the lee of the island.

The Berries

Outside of the protection of land the wind increased significantly providing us with an ever increasing spirited sail. We were sailing south southeast. Our destination Great Stirrup Island. When the sun climbed over the horizon we had sailed completely out of the lee of Grand Bahama. Accordingly the wind increased to 25 knots right on the beam with a long rolling six to eight foot pleasant ocean swell from port aft with the wave train speed of about three knots. These are the conditions that Quest was built for. The Bayfield 36 is a stout cutter rigged cruiser with a very compact sail plan. The cutter rig with its small main and considerable foresail area made her a dream to sail for beginners in ocean conditions. Her porpoise-shaped bottom excelled at slicing diagonally across long high crested ocean swells. The long heavy keel added considerable stability and perfect tracking to an already well balanced rig. In these perfect conditions, Quest needed very little trimming. It wasn't necessary to trim for maximum speed. We trimmed for safety. With the autopilot set and holding within half of a degree on either side of our rhumb line our duties became passive. On our straight line passage of twelve hours with no deviation we had ample opportunity to enjoy the solitude and splendor of being in a small boat in a big tropical ocean.

While waiting for a high spring tide at Running Mon I devised a culinary experiment which I hoped would overcome an inadequacy in our marine stove. Not all overpriced marine gear is perfect. The oven in our marine stove was no more than a shiny Stainless Steel Easy-Bake oven. On too many occasions I had tried to cook a proper calzone. The best our oven could muster was a burnt on the outside, raw on the inside inedible mess. Our oven was more suited as a space heater than a baking appliance. There had to be a way to cook a calzone. If there was a way it would have to be on the stove top not in the oven.

The day before our departure Wendy and I walked to the grocery store in Freeport to purchase fresh produce. As I turned the cart down a sparsely populated kitchen gadget aisle my eyes stopped on a small display of twelve inch nonstick frying pans on sale. Wendy observed me hesitating at the pans.

"Thinking about throwing out that wreck of a frying pan?" she asked.

"Not exactly, I was thinking that if we bought two of these identical pans then I could flip one pan over and match it to a bottom pan. That would create a lid for the bottom pan."

I demonstrated.

"Why don't you just buy a lid?" she asked.

"A lid won't serve the purpose. The plan at this stage is to make about two pounds of good yeasty dough, roll half the dough flat and form it to the bottom of the first greased pan. Grease the other pan and place the ingredients: broccoli, mushrooms, onions, mozzarella, parmesan, tomato sauce and herbs into the bottom pie shell. Then roll out the second half of the dough, gently place it over the mounded ingredients and seal the edges. It will form a pie of sorts. The top pan will be placed over the bottom pan to keep in the heat. When the bottom crust is cooked I will hold the top and bottom pans together with a kitchen towel and flip both pans over at the same time and cook the other side."

"Then it's going to be like a big round calzone?" she asked.

"No, it's going to be a gourmet hobo lunch pie." The name didn't strike Wendy favorably.

"How about a calzone in a pan?" she offered.

"How about a Panzone!" I said.

Generally, innovations like the Panzone that exist as vague notions and reside exclusively in the imagination need to gestate before they can be brought into the world. Around mid day of our sail while I was digesting a light lunch, I became increasingly curious about exactly how the concept of the Panzone would take form.

"We have plenty of time until we make our waypoint" I said to Wendy. "I'm going to start the Panzone."

Wendy in a moment of disbelief stared at the ceiling of the hardtop and said "You're going to fry onions, cook broccoli, and make dough in eight foot seas?"

"Don't panic" I said. "I'm going to do the easy part. I'm just starting the dough. When the dough is finished I will cold proof it in the fridge over night."

"OK" she shrugged.

I assembled the ingredients for the dough. A common method of starting dough is with a poolish. A poolish is water and sugar at about 100 degrees Fahrenheit mixed with yeast and about half the flour. This batter is then allowed to ferment. After an hour in the tropical heat the poolish was foamy with a good earthy smell. I brought the bowl below and mixed in the remaining flour, salt, a bit of olive oil, oregano and basil and worked it into a rough ball. I returned to the cockpit and placed the bowl of dough on the bench beside me to proof. Sailing on a straight rhumb line with a heavy cruiser requires boat and crew to always work as a tight unit. Quest cruised. I slept.

After resting the dough for about an hour, I went below and dropped the dough on a slab of Corian affixed to the top of the galley stove and began a twenty minute knead. While I knead dough I always enjoy watching the raw dough take form and change texture. I stared at the rhythmic motion of the dough being pressed and pushed into the kneading board and from hand to hand. But as I continued to stare at the ball of dough I noticed that the dotted pattern on the Corian kneading board began to shift slightly in my peripheral vision. I was getting seasick. All the subtle early signs were there. I looked into the cabin. The room was spinning slowly. Mal de mar is very difficult to control once it takes a firm hold. This was the time to act.

"First mate" I said to Wendy through the companionway door. "I'm taking half a Scopace."

Before this fast acting and very potent medication took effect I lay on the settee trying to wish away my sea sickness. Scopace is an orally administered dose of Scopolamine, the same active ingredient of the Scopolamine patch. I ground the very bitter Scopace into a paste between my teeth, swallowed it with a cup of tea and lay back down. The more common scopolamine patch requires many hours to be effective. It is an agonizingly slow release method. The effects from Scopace are felt almost immediately. Within fifteen minutes I was feeling good enough to finish the kneading. But when I got back to kneading the dough ball it almost immediately began to swim about the kneading board. I was ready for the other half of the Scopace. I crunched the other half and stretched out in the cockpit.

Our purposeful departure from Running Mon Marina at 2 AM allowed us to take full advantage of an exceptionally high spring tide. The early departure also gave us the optimal arrival time at Great Stirrup Island. When sailing the Bahamas it is critical when navigating an unknown entrance that the helmsman must always have the sun over his shoulder and not in his eyes. If the sun is in his eyes then the sunlight reflects off the water and completely obscures the subtle color changes at the varying depths. It is normal practice 'to read the water' by observing the delicate changes of inky blues, cerulean blues, robin egg blues, powder blues, sandy white blues. If there are grasses on the bottom there will be a whole spectrum of aquamarines and emeralds.

Our GPS brought us to a point just outside the 75 foot wide channel into Great Stirrup. Guided by the hallucinatory influence of scopolamine I made my first practical attempt at reading the depths of the water by observing these subtle color changes. The darker blues marked the center of the channel. As the channel became shallower at the sides, the color of the water changed gradually to lighter and lighter shades of powder blue. The strong currents that form the channels through the coral rock over the millennia in the Bahamas have not always carved perfectly straight channels. This is the primary reason why a prudent sailor in the Bahamas will always enter cuts with the sun over his shoulder. This will give him the advantage of seeing the color of the water and sticking closely to the channel.

Quest's draft was six feet. There aren't many places in the Berry's with more than four feet of water. Our anchoring choice in this huge one mile wide bay was a small area just behind Goat Cay with twenty feet of water.

Of greater concern than our options for anchoring was the weather system that was about to pass through the Bahamas. Our weather analysis from the previous day placed a southerly moving cold front passing over our location around midnight. When the front blew through, the wind would swing one hundred and eighty degrees from a northerly direction to directly south. The estimated wind strength after the front passed would be in the twenty-five to thirty knot range. When the wind did swing it would funnel directly through the entrance making our snug anchorage into a choppy roadstead.

We laid out plenty of chain. We were going to need plenty of holding power when the front hit us in the middle of the night.

The islands that comprise the entire Bahama chain are just rocky sandy bumps in the Atlantic Ocean. They provide no resistance or shelter from the cold fronts that sweep in from North America. The only consequential benefit of being at the mercy of every storm is that the cold front's arrival is highly predictable. At exactly 1:30 AM the north wind slackened and then went dead calm. I woke and went on deck. The anchor chain was hanging loose. Quest was swinging in every direction. Within twenty minutes there was the slightest breath of air from the southeast coming straight from the entrance of the huge bay. Over the next two hours the wind increased to a steady 25 to 30 knots. Although the wind was formidable we had more than enough scope to handle the breeze. But as a result of the change in wind direction Quest's stern had swung to within one hundred feet of the rock pile known as Goat Cay. We had little choice but to accept this lee shore scenario. I went back to my bunk and considered that within a couple of hours the ocean swell would be pushing right through the entrance making our anchorage a windy bumpy ride.

By dawn the surface of our anchorage looked like the inside of a washing machine. During the night I had twice been pitched from my bunk by the constant rolling. I dragged my mattress onto the cabin floor and wedged my hips between the saloon table and the settee. When I awoke I gathered my strength and sat in the cockpit. In the middle of my haze I remembered the big ball of dough and a pound of broccoli thawing in the fridge. Just the thought of food made me queasy. I opened the Scopace bottle and swallowed a full dose. Although the rolling and pitching increased in strength the Scopace dramatically reduced my symptoms. In a Scopolamine fog I chopped and fried two onions, steamed the broccoli, grated the two cheeses then placed all of the ingredients back in the fridge where they couldn't roll about the cabin.

Surprisingly enough, frying the onions didn't set off another attack of Mal de Mar, nor did grating the parmesan. But the memory of handling the dough the previous day was lingering in my mind. As I laid the rolling pin on the ball of dough to form the top crust, I almost immediately felt sick. I sat down in the fresh air of the cockpit to pull myself together. I turned the instruments on. The wind was howling steady at around thirty knots coming straight through the entrance and carrying what seemed like half the Atlantic with it. I took another half a Scopace and went back to the job of building the Panzone. I finished the top crust, oiled the bottom pan and formed the dough to the top edge of the pan. I coated the dough with a wash of marinara sauce and layered all the ingredients one at a time.

While I was placing the top crust on top of the ingredients Wendy came up to me and asked "Do you feel a vibration?"

"Vibration?" I laughed. "You've got to be kidding. I'm in Ixtlan. I can't feel anything above my heels."

"Well there is definitely a vibration in the cockpit" she said.

"I'll check after I turn the pan on" I mumbled incoherently.

I placed the top crust over the cheese and vegetables, folded and sealed the edges and placed the second greased pan on top. I had just tightened the fiddles and started the burner when I began to feel a slight vibration. I bumped my way through the companionway.

The Berries

"Where is that vibration coming from?" I asked Wendy.

"It seems to be coming from the back of the boat somewhere."

We sat and listened for a few moments. It was coming from everywhere. Then the hardtop began to rattle mildly, the shaking became violent. I searched everywhere. I couldn't find the source of the vibration.

"The wind generator, it's got to be the wind generator" I said to Wendy.

The wind generator was bolted directly to the hardtop. I didn't have to get close to the generator to see that it was shaking madly. I looked around for a boat hook and very carefully swung the generator around in the opposite direction of the wind to feather the blades. I felt the housing. It was hot. I tied the blades down with a short piece of line so that it couldn't rotate. The generator was designed with an automatic brake to slow the rotation of the blades if the wind grew too strong. It normally worked quite well. A sustained 30 knot wind gusting to 35 knots was just too much for the brake.

With the wind generator under control I sat down to catch my breath. Oh no, I said to myself, the Panzone! I jumped through the companionway into the galley and pushed a spatula under the Panzone. It was really coming along. The bottom was a golden brown. I held the two pans together with a kitchen towel and flipped them over exposing the uncooked side to the burner. After performing the tricky Panzone flip maneuver I felt a flush of confidence. I bet I could turn the wind generator back on. If I restarted the wind generator then I could use the excess electrical power to run the watermaker. I crawled on top of the hard top and released the tether that was holding the blades from rotating. As I rocked and swayed unsteadily on the hardtop I looked out at the entrance of the anchorage.

"Wendy you got to come see this. This has got to be the biggest whale in the world."

Wendy ran through the companionway in time to get a perfect view of the eight hundred foot long, one hundred and fifty foot high, white whale, its larger than life dimensions strongly contrasted against an island that is only eight feet high. The whale of a cruise ship slowly crept past the harbor entrance and picked up a deep water mooring a quarter a mile off their private beach just north of our anchorage. Within ten minutes of picking up the mooring, all passengers that weren't currently eating, about to eat, or had just eaten were transported to Fantasy Island for a day of high throttle water sports. For two hours our rough and rolly anchorage was recreated into a cruise ship director's dream world by seventy-five enthusiastic jet skiers racing at full throttle around the anchorage in single file behind their Bahamian handlers.

Quest was the only buoy in the anchorage. It was the target for all curious adrenaline saturated jet skiers. The jet skis each had a time limit of approximately thirty minutes. There were a lot of eager enthusiasts. Wave after wave of jet skiers left the beach at timed intervals. They headed directly toward Quest. They circled Quest five times within easy reach of a boathook, raced about the anchorage for fifteen minutes, circled Quest five more times and returned to the beach. This pattern repeated for several hours until one blast from the ship's horn brought the party to an end. With an end to the water sport a welcome peace returned to the anchorage. After thirty minutes, two blasts from the cruise ship's horn signaled her departure. She was gone without a trace.

They came. They wreaked havoc. They left. The Panzone experiment proved to be an unqualified success. I removed the top pan from the Panzone and quickly turned it over onto the kneading board and cut into it. It was beautiful, a thin golden crust on the outside with plenty of cheese and vegetables. Quest and crew remained in the anchorage for another three days to ride out the rest of the storm in solitude. The oven was officially decommissioned without ceremony, never to be used again.

Seventeen

Nassau Shakedown

It was difficult to engender warm feelings for Great Stirrup Island as we pulled up anchor and sailed away. It was a barren rocky outcropping with an average elevation of eight feet. The desert like environment offered only a sparse existence for the reptilian population. From a boating perspective the anchorage is far too exposed. It served us adequately as a roadstead providing us moderate shelter for several days during a pretty good blow. 'Let's get out of here!'

In order to return a degree of calm to our lives it was necessary to leave the turbulence of Great Stirrup Island and seek shelter twenty-five miles south in Devil's Cay. Our first opportunity was a one-day weather window between the cold front that had raised the white caps at Great Stirrup and given us our first good shakedown. The next cold front was due in thirty hours.

We left Great Stirrup at dawn and fought head seas and a stout breeze right on the nose, arriving at the entrance of Devil's Cay seven hours later. Devil's was a complete contrast to Great Stirrup. Great Stirrup was a vast one mile wide open roadstead at the mercy of every weather anomaly. Devil's was tiny in comparison. It was only large enough to anchor several small yachts at once. The island's geology was identical to the majority of the small Bahama islands. Narrow craggy outcroppings of sharp rocks formed the short spine of the islands with a thin fringe of sand where the rock met sea. We found a mooring between two heavy draft boats and securely dug in the anchor. Being surrounded by the short rocky lifeless walls of the island gave us more of a sense of being behind a breakwall than the embrace of a tropical island.

The predicted cold front was expected in the wee hours of the next morning. With the approach of the front the wind would slacken from northwest then go calm. The calm would last an hour; the wind would then veer one hundred and eighty degrees and blast in from south east. With foreknowledge of this very predictable weather pattern in mind we moored in the approximate center of this three hundred foot wide oval shaped anchorage with one hundred and twenty-five feet of chain. This placed the stern very close to shore. But when Quest swung with the sudden abrupt wind change from the approaching front her aft would swing and should come to rest within thirty feet of the opposite rocky shore line. This was theory.

I was sound asleep when the front passed over. The winds that accompany weather systems blasting through the Bahamas in the early winter are formidable. The leading edge of the front has the ferocity of a squall with thirty-five knot winds gusting to forty. Devil's Cay would provide shelter from the ocean swell. It was so small and low that it gave little resistance to the wind.

Quest and Crew

Our brief and thoroughly uncomfortable visit to Great Stirrup had accomplished a very tangible result. It set the standard for discomfort while anchored. The experience also gave me my permanent sea legs. When the front did come driving through Devil's Cay, it wasn't the howling of the wind that awoke me at 4:30 AM. It wasn't even the mild rolling in the anchorage. It was an intensely bright white light.

"Turn off the lights and go back to bed" I said to Wendy as I pulled the sheets over my head.

"You turn off the lights, I didn't turn them on" she muttered.

I reached up to the cabin light and fumbled for the switch with eyes closed. What was going on? The switch was off. I opened my eyes and the entire interior of Quest was lit up like daylight and the light was coming from outside. Had I slept that long? I checked the clock. It wasn't even five o'clock yet. I pulled on a pair of shorts and went into the cockpit. What a scene of absolute mayhem; the boats that were anchored on our port and starboard side had all of their mast and aft floodlights blasting.

The lights were illuminating a very potentially threatening scene. When the wind swung in the middle of the night all three boats had swung in unison to the opposite shore of the anchorage as expected. The immediate danger to Quest was that the wind was blowing with sufficient strength to pull most of the slack out of the anchor chain. Our stern was now ten feet from shore. I turned on the Yanmar and I didn't wait for it to warm up. I threw it into gear and inched forward taking the strain off the ground tackle. Taking a cue from my neighbors I turned on all my flood lights.

The instruments gave me a reading of 35 knots with an occasional 45 knot gust. The wind increased steadily. The crews of the three boats sat and waited in their cockpits, engines revving, our fates resting on the holding power of our anchors. There was no solace knowing that the worst was almost over, that we were right on the leading edge of the front and we would be reprieved when the wind would slacken to 25 knots within hours. Beaching was one of the possibilities that I contemplated sitting in the cockpit. Just one bit of bad luck, one weak piece of gear between the three boats and it would be all over. A beached boat under $150,000 on a remote Bahama island is pretty much a lost cause, a financial write off. It has no salvage value except for the parts that can be cannibalized or plundered.

We could only wait and hope that the engine salt water cooling intake didn't suck up enough sand to destroy the impellor and cause the engine to overheat or that the ground tackle held. The minutes dragged. By early dawn the worst of the front passed. The wind slackened to a comfortable 25 knots. We had survived another teeth clenching, adrenaline saturated encounter with the winter cold front. The experience further tested our resolve to push south. Our next destination would be the Exumas, a chain of islands stretching south of Nassau.

After the storm, the swells that eventually made their way into Devil's Cay encouraged us with every roll of the hull to make our departure. It was time to press on to

191

Nassau, New Providence Island, and the home of most of the Bahamas population, a population that would initiate us into some of the finer points of Caribbean cruising. Nassau was a straight forward sail almost due south in mild ocean conditions for about fifty miles. The first contrast between the Berrys and New Providence Island for a sailor is the presence of two freshly painted jumbo buoys a half mile out to sea. We would soon learn two interesting facts that made these buoys very special. The first was that they were the only two well-maintained all-weather lighted buoys in the Bahamas and the second was that they were maintained by the US Coast Guard for the dedicated purpose of keeping the fleet of cruise ships in the channel.

We sailed through the buoys and entered a different world. We had about thirty minutes to find dockage on New Providence Island. It was a week before Christmas; space could be tight. We would take what we could get. I hailed Nassau Yacht Haven marina. Nassau's sailboat marinas are clustered midway along the channel between New Providence Island and Paradise Island. The docks are at right angles to a strong current that blasts through the channel. The cruising guides were quite specific that it would be most advantageous to enter the docks at slack tide. We had missed this opportunity by about three hours. The next best scenario was to attempt to dock during a full ebbing current into a south facing slip. This would allow me to motor into the current. The last and worst possibility was to dock with the current pushing directly on the stern. The final scenario presented the interesting and often entertaining maneuver of stopping a sailboat with the current hard on the stern. One of the interesting design features of Bayfield sailboats is that they have well defined limitations while maneuvering in reverse. In the simplest of terms, Quest stubbornly resists any attempts to back up. Quest would on occasion behave but it wasn't because I was trying.

"Nassau Yacht Haven, this is the sailing vessel Quest."

"Good day, this is Nassau Yacht Haven."

"Quest here; do you have any slips available?"

"Yes mon, we got plenty slip."

"Do you have any docks facing south into the current?" I asked.

"Current good mon."

I looked at Wendy. Describing a 4.5 knot cross-current blasting through the docks as good seemed a bit cavalier, even for the Bahamas. I keyed the microphone.

"Did you say that the current was good?"

"Current very good, mon. No problem with current, it 110, 50 cycle. Real good current!"

Wendy and I slid back into the cockpit cushions and broke up. 'What we have here is a failure to communicate'. If the dock boy and I could be that far off on the current then I better double check on the slip assignment. I looked at the numbered layout of the marina in my cruising guide.

"Please give me the number of the slip" I requested.

With a good humored laugh he said "Don't worry

bout number. I stand on end on dock and catch lines. You see me."

"Is he being obtuse?" I asked Wendy.

"Just naturally obtuse" she replied.

We had about half an hour before we would enter the marina. Just enough time to extract a few choice dry facts about our host country. I scanned through a few pages of documents on the computer. We were entering the capital city of one of the few countries in the world that defy, and define, the laws of economics. The Bahamas make no pretense of being more than a 500 mile beached coral reef unsuited for agriculture. Four hundred seventy-three goats, 833 chickens and 250 pet tomato plants compete on a vast archipelago of islands that does not have enough water to encourage life.

First observations could place the Bahamas in the category of a struggling third world country. But dig just a little deeper. The Bahamas have no income tax, no corporate tax, no capital gains tax, and no sales tax. The citizenry, especially on the out islands, are living in poverty. So often our first impressions offer only a glimpse of reality. In the Bahamas a glimpse of reality is about all that you are going to get. In truth the Bahamas are an economic powerhouse that defies gravity. The Bahamas per capita income has been in the top ten of all nations of the world for many, many years. One of the richest countries in the world has no military and they depend on foreign aid for their smorgasbord of social programs. It is a nation of a thousand islands that stretches for hundreds of miles yet they do not recognize the need for navigational aids.

As we sailed closer to Nassau with the incredibly glittering opulence of Atlantis on our left and the secret vaults of Nassau on our right, it was my pleasure to observe this phenomenon of wealth. I would not be briefed by the Prime Minister or the American ambassador. I was counting on the friendly and unfettered common man on the street to graciously educate a foreigner on the local perspective.

We made our approach to the marina. The dock boy waved us to a slip.

"You're supposed to be on the north side of the docks" I yelled from the cockpit.

"No!, dis yo slip, skipper."

I had to drop Plan A and pick up Plan D. I had to think quickly and reorient myself to the strong current that would now be pushing us with considerable force into the slip. Hopefully, Quest's reverse wouldn't fail me. When I got within twenty feet of the dock about six cruisers watching our approach sensed disaster. They ran over and frantically grabbed the mooring line from Wendy. It wasn't the smoothest landing but there was no paint chipped. The most gregarious of the cruisers reached over the gunwales and shook my hand.

"Not a bad docking. It must be nice to have a reverse that works so well. Now I know why you asked for a slip with the current on your stern."

I shrugged.

"I'm just kidding" he said. "When the current is really bad, the dock boy always, and I mean always, sends the new fish to the worst docks. Welcome to Nassau."

Following our exciting arrival in Nassau we set off to discover the land of plenty.

"Let's go to the cruise ship docks and watch the three whales we passed this morning disgorge" I said to Wendy.

"Sounds very appetizing" Wendy said.

We flagged down the next municipal bus heading for old down town Nassau. During the brief ride we passed clusters of jewelry merchants hocking the finest gems in the world, diamonds, emeralds, and sapphires suitable for royalty but affordable by the masses. We passed row upon row of duty free liquor and tobacco stores all selling the same liquor and Cuban cigars. Arriving at the cruise ship docks we disembarked from the four wheeled bone shaker.

"So where is everybody?" I said to a group of taxi drivers sitting under the shade of a quaint banyan tree.

He looked at his wrist which lacked any type of time piece and said "They're eating!" Judging by the snickers and leg-slapping from his merry band of gnomes, the joker possessed insider information.

"When do they stop eating?" I asked.

"When food gone...they fall off boat in twenty minutes" he replied.

Roars of laughter followed the cabbies deadpan delivery.

"Do you mind if I ask you a question?" I said.

"You want to know where the beach is, right?" he laughed.

"No... not really. Can you tell me why a six-pack of

beer costs twenty dollars and a bag of Doritos costs eight bucks?"

Four of the drivers that had been playing checkers abruptly stopped and stood up. The comedian ring leader became quiet and stone faced. The silence became menacing. Three seconds seemed like five minutes. Just when I was about to execute a speedy retreat, all seven of my new buddies started talking at the same time. The overlapping conversations were impossible to follow.

Decorum was restored when the comedian driver put up his hand and shouted "Shut up. I tell him. Look, we pay same as you for a can of beer. Everything expensive in Bahamas and we get paid nothing. Look at us. We just get poorer, mon. That no joke."

"But the Bahamas is one of the richest countries in the world" I replied.

He looked me in the eye and said "This country has rich politicians that take and take, they no more than bandits. They would sell us if they could."

"What government isn't corrupt?" I asked.

"All corrupt…but not every body have world class thieves like us." A volley of laughter followed. He continued uninterrupted. "It all so simple; banking, money, money, money. Drug running, pharmaceuticals, and none of them pay taxes. This country big wealthy mess. And the little man get nothing but one of the highest murder rates in the world. They get big house on hill with swimming pool. We get what runs down hill. And it get worse every year!"

"Stay right here. I'll be right back" I said.

Wendy and I went across the street to a bar and bought two six packs of Bud and two bags of Doritos. I placed the goodies under the banyan tree.

"Sure, mon. We drink your beer."

Our host popped a can and toasted our health.

"The question still remains" I said. "Why does a can of beer cost three dollars?"

"Didn't I tell you? There are many hungry thieves to feed." He raised his right hand. "One, excise taxes. Two, bribes to Customs, bribes to the port official, bribes to police. Corruption is a beer can that never goes empty" he laughed as he swigged the last bit of the beer and tossed the can. But you know what?" He pointed at the cruise ships. "That's why a can of beer costs three bucks. They pay three bucks for cold beer and don't complain. But look at you, sharp dresser. Go back to your boat, Skipper. Nobody gonna get rich off you."

The three cruise ships gave a single blast on their horns signaling the beginning of disgorging. Our new friend snapped his happy face back on.

"Mon, don't ask so many questions, it give you headaches. Now OUR time to make money. Look, the money falling outta their pockets."

Within moments the cruise ship began disembarking their passengers, not one at a time, not even two at a time. From the distance of a quarter mile, the passengers looked like a multi-colored stream of toothpaste getting squeezed out of the cruise ships. As they proceeded down the long dock in tightly formed ranks they slowly made their way through Customs. In a matter of minutes the square was overrun with a sunburned horde of typical American cruise ship passengers seeking a glimpse of that old Bahama style and any handy bargain rubies that might be available.

In a few hours the ship's horn would sound to signal the passengers to return to their eight story snack bar. In the brief time that the passengers were on the island, the life supporting currency that keeps the Bahamas solvent would flow from tourists' credit cards to the bank accounts of the world. I took the cabbie's advice and quit asking stupid questions. The Bahamas has too many years of developing secrecy for one cruiser to understand the price of beer.

Eighteen

Enter the Exumas

We silently maneuvered Quest south on a quiet Sunday morning while the bankers and gem merchants slept or partied. Depending on their individual shipboard schedules, the cruise ship passengers enjoyed their first meal of the day or last leftovers from the previous evening buffet. Our heading was Allan's Cay, the first island in the Exumas.

To a resident of New Providence Island, Nassau is the center of the Bahamas. To the rest of the people inhabiting the sprawling archipelago of Bahamian islands, Nassau is just a dot on the map where their weekly mail boat originates then returns. The pace of life on the thousands of out islands is slow. Viewed from the quick pace of Nassau the remote out-islands are unchanging, static. To the lucky few in Nassau who live and harvest wealth on New Providence Island it is the crown jewel of the Bahamas. For the rest of the unprivileged out-island dwellers, Nassau is an emerald city. It lures many. It frightens others. But to most of the out islanders it is not the crown jewel of the Bahamas. In contrast to New Providence Island the wealth of the out islanders is not contained by vault and password. It is visible and available to everyone. It is the bountiful treasure of thousands of picturesque islands scattered across an azure sea.

As we sailed south into the Exumas the dazzle, sparkle and allure of the city/state/island of New Providence vanished like a dream before we were over the horizon. What remained in our minds were the sketchy remnants of one of the world's classic enigmas. One could stroll the old streets of Nassau for years, taking the forced charm of a city which exists solely to entertain the transient wealthy pleasure-seekers. An observant tourist would take delight and pleasure in seeing the charm of the old colonial houses. They would enjoy the hospitality of fiercely competitive merchants. Few tourists would be aware or even vaguely interested in the nature of the business that takes place twenty-four hours a day behind the picturesque pink and turquoise wall of the historic buildings. With key or password all secrets are safe within banks of sterling reputation. Banks with centuries old pedigrees sit baking in the Bahamian sun as billions of dollars per second are transferred into accounts, washed, sanitized and rerouted to banks in every corner of the world. The fine clockwork of the international banking machine is as quiet as a Swiss watch.

As we were leaving our slip for the Exumas the charter boat captain that was moored beside us during our stay cast off our lines.

"Any parting words of wisdom?" I asked as we motored into the stream.

"Beware, the Exumas are mined!" he shouted.

"The Exumas are yours?" I shouted and shrugged.

"The Exumas are mined" he said again.

This time he squeezed his hands tightly together then spread them apart quickly miming an explosion. Wendy and I looked at each other.

"What is he getting at?" Wendy asked.

I said "He's Australian. I think it's sarcasm."

We had arrived in Nassau three days before and our first communication with the island was a cryptic and undecipherable message from a dock boy. On departure we took away with us an equally confusing message from a fellow member of the boating community.

"How dramatic!" I said.

"They don't go in much for hellos and goodbyes here" added Wendy.

It wasn't until we were well south and I had the chart for the North Exumas laid out that I finally got the joke. The charter boat captain was right. The approach to the Exumas is mined. There is no direct route from Nassau to our first stop in the Exumas without running a dangerous gauntlet of coral heads. Coral in general is composed of the skeletons secreted by various anthozoans. These tiny creatures are responsible for the millions of miles of coral reefs that stretch around the planet in tropical waters. A variant of the coral reef is the coral head which could be thought of as a single polyp or spike upward from a coral reef. As we approached the Exumas our charts warned of an immense unmarked field of coral heads stretching across our path. The charts warned us. The charter captain warned us. The cruising guide was even more clear: 'Danger…only enter the coral head field with the sun over your shoulder and it is highly advisable to station a capable crew member at the bow to sight for coral heads!' We were sailing on a mild reach with full sail in a crystal blue sea.

"You better go to the bow and spot for coral heads" I said to Wendy.

"What do they look like?"

"Just look for any submerged obstructions and warn me as soon as you see something" I said.

In these shallow waters the heads have a base of fifteen feet across on the bottom and grow up in a conical shape until they are a foot or two below sea level. They are as hard as concrete and a light brush with one can tear the bottom out of any boat. For about five miles Wendy would be our eyes. When we approached a particularly populated coral head field Wendy started yelling out.

"There's one, there's two more over there."

I gritted my teeth. "Look Wendy this isn't Marine Park. Just tell me when there is a head in our path."

She calmed down and started to look along our course.

"Right" she screamed and waved her arms in both directions.

I spun the wheel. The stern of Quest missed the coral head by three feet.

"Left, Left LEFT!"

I turned hard to port and we sailed between heads. This was getting exciting but stressful. For a good hour as we picked our way through the field, teamwork and four eyes, quick reflexes, and adrenalin kept Quest safe.

The Exumas are an archipelago that stretches 150 miles southeast of Nassau. Thousands of islands varying in size from a parking lot to islands the size of Manhattan form a very compact and tight line of demarcation between the fury of the North Atlantic and the calmness of the Exuma banks.

Our approach to Allen's Cay was routine. Allen's Cay is a collective of three different islands that form a very snug secure anchorage. The narrow gaps between the islands allow the tidal waters to pass. Once a day the millions upon millions of gallons of tidal waters from the Atlantic are forced through the gaps created by the islands. Then once a day the process reverses and the Bahama Banks water is forced between the islands. This sets up tremendous currents between the islands which scour a channel between the closely spaced islands.

A boat anchored between the islands is subjected twice a day to a very significant current reversal. You will go to sleep facing one direction and probably wake up facing another. A style referred to as Bahama anchoring can prevent the vessel from swinging in this current reversal. The simplest form of Bahama Anchoring is to set a bow anchor, then dinghy behind the boat and set a second bow anchor. The boat will be held by the first bow anchor when the current is on the bow and when the current reverses the second anchor will hold the boat. The Americans and Europeans who make up the vast majority of yachts in the Bahamas do not embrace this type of anchoring. Whether due to ignorance or stubbornness they seem content to swing one hundred and eighty degrees at anchor with every tidal change. When many boats are swinging on their anchor twice a day it seriously restricts the number of boats that an anchorage can hold. If a yacht has fifty feet of rode played out then over the course of twenty four hours the boat needs one hundred feet of anchorage to make a complete arc or in most cases a full circle.

Herein lay the difficult situation that faced us when entering the anchorage at Allen's Cay. A quick survey of the waters indicated that there was a spot to anchor directly in front of a charter boat. When dealing with charter boats it is common practice to be cautious and not assume any level of boating proficiency. I hailed the charter boat in front of me. The boat stern was pointing right at me so when we swung at current reversal I would need the same amount of rode as he had. The name on the stern was Simpatico.

"Simpatico, come back!" I called.

"This is the captain of Simpatico" he replied.

"Hey Wendy we got a real captain on board the charter." I thumbed the mike. "This is Quest, the boat directly behind you. I am anchoring and I would like to know how much rode you have out."

"I put it all out."

Wendy and I looked at each other.

"What exactly is all of it?" I queried.

"I don't know" he said. "The people at Moorings Charters told us to put out all our anchor rode."

"Well what do you think you have out?" I asked.

"Wait a minute I'll check" he said. "Yes, the booklet says we have two hundred feet of rode."

"You do know that you are in nine feet of water?" I asked.

"Yes nine feet under the keel, Captain, that is correct" came his reply.

There was no point in wasting time teaching him how to anchor. In nine feet of water he should have had about fifty feet of rode. This was a crowded anchorage. Two hundred feet of rode swinging in a 360 degree arc takes up sixteen times the anchorage that fifty feet would have occupied. Putting out 200 feet of rode in a crowded anchorage is a telling demonstration of one's lack of boating knowledge. It is also about as rude a move as one can make. I played out 200 feet of rode, cursed the charter boat industry and sat down for a beer.

The anchorage was one of the best that we had found in the Bahamas up to that point. There was Allen's Cay to the west, Leaf Cay to the east and SW Allen's Cay directly south. We were anchored roughly in the center of these islands. With 200 feet of rode we could have withstood a hurricane. The topology and make up of the islands was straight Bahama style. Short rocky outcroppings fringed by a tiny beach of coral sand describe the islands that seem to rise out of a magnificent tropical blue sea. At a quick glance the islands seemed sparsely vegetated as if they hadn't seen any rain since the last hurricane season. The dryness and hostility of the environment did not create a mental image of an island paradise. Looking out onto the bleakness gave us the impression that it was completely void of life. The following day our explorations would school us on the variety of life that can flourish in places so apparently hostile. The animals were there and they were easy to find. You just have to know where to look.

Our first evening at Allens Cay was smooth and tranquil. The Atlantic ceaselessly pounded the windward coast of the island. The three small islands were situated in perfect formation to block the waves and keep the waters of the anchorage smooth. This was a more than welcome experience after the previous month of enduring anchoring hell, holed up in roadsteads so rolly that you felt like you were in a Pacific typhoon. I rose from my bunk the next morning and climbed to the cockpit to survey the anchorage. The charter boat had left in the early morning. This was a pleasant development. I would pull up about 150 feet of anchor rode after breakfast. With life, and life on boats, it isn't the known that will cause all the grief. Unknown to me, a major Australian storm was making its way through the cut into the anchorage. While preparing the morning meal for Wendy and me there came a rather aggressive banging on the stern of the boat, followed by several gravelly sounding hellos barked out in a rural Australian accent. With a pan in one hand I came out on deck. Without a word of introduction the stranger began his rapid, semi-coherent verbal attack.

"I have been trying to get you on the VHF for an hour" he said.

"I generally turn off the VHF so people won't annoy me" I joked.

Not being in a joking mood he launched at me again. "How much rode do you have out?" he growled.

"Two hundred feet" I mumbled quietly.

Stand back, he is about to blow. I endured two minutes of slanderous insults regarding my boating skills, my mother, his sainted mother and my ignorance of marine courtesy. Ignoring his abuse I turned on the engine and pulled in 150 feet of rode. The Australian held onto the top sides of Quest firing insults over the gunwales the entire time. I returned to my breakfast. The Australian motored away and calmness returned.

With breakfast digested it was time to explore Allens, Leaf and SW Allens Cays. We piled into the dinghy. But first we paid a visit to the argumentative Australian. After a brief explanation why I let out two hundred feet of rode, he handed me the traditional Australian breakfast beverage, a big can of beer. We drank; we swapped charter boat horror stories for a time. He was a delivery captain bringing a sizable yacht to Miami from the Virgins. He had sailed overnight to Allens Cay. He was not 'at his best' when he approached us that morning. We left as friends and agreed to have a few beers at sundown.

Wendy and I set off to see what other wildlife the Islands had to offer. When we came within a hundred feet of SW Allens Cay, Wendy looked back and indicated by mad gesturing to stop the dinghy.

"Did you see that?" she said.

"What?" I asked.

"There are black blobs crawling all over the island" she shouted.

Sure enough the island had hundreds of grey objects about the size of small dogs crawling over the beach. I put the engine back in gear and approached. As we got closer we could make out the shapes of huge lizards.

"Let's get out of here" she said.

"Hold on" I said. "This is better than the Galapagos."

I beached the dinghy. The monster lizards didn't move an inch. We walked onto the small sandy beach. The lizard residents paid no attention. The occasional pair of lizards sparred in the glaring sunlight. Larger lizards brunched on their smaller more vulnerable relatives. The remaining population seemed to be content to bask in the heat of the sand. They were so thick on the beach that we were constantly stepping over them. There were small lizards and there were ones as big as Great Danes. We took hundreds of photos. We walked stealthily. We didn't make any abrupt movements. It is disconcerting to be outnumbered by thousands of creatures that could take your leg off with one bite.

The intrusion into their sanctuary concluded in a completely peaceful manner. After passing through the gauntlet of startling hissing reptiles we crossed the spine of this tiny craggy island which was about one hundred feet across. The windward shore was completely different from the shore where we had beached the dinghy. It seemed much more hostile and bleak than the beach side. The shore line was a composition of jagged edged coral rock with numerous tidal pools arranged along the shoreline like a necklace. This side of the island was so uninviting that even the lizards stayed away. The evidence that this side of the island was exposed to the force of the Atlantic was evident in every crag and sculptured outcropping.

Quest and Crew

Although this side of the island was obviously inhospitable to lizards, it was heaven for Wendy and me. We made our way down to the shore line carefully avoiding the sharp edged coral rock. We removed our clothes and eased ourselves into a tidal pool no bigger than a Jacuzzi for two. Warmed by the sun the small pools of water were a pleasant bathtub temperature. We hadn't taken a decent wash in warm water in weeks. As we soaked we spoke and joked about many things. We laughed about man eating lizards, quick to anger Australians, the dangers that lurk in the cockpits of charter boats. Mostly we spoke of an adventure that had barely begun. On that Christmas Eve in the middle of the Bahamas there was nothing mentioned of the trials and tests of our courage and stamina that were inevitably awaiting us. On that day, our most cherished Christmas gift of all was a warm tidal pool and a faith in Quest and ourselves that was completely non-denominational.

View photographs of the Exumas as well as satellite views of the islands and Quest's route at www.questandcrew.com

Nineteen

Norman's Cay

Even an island covered with friendly man-eating lizards can lose its appeal after a few days. It was time to sail south to Norman's Cay. Norman's is an island with a group of smaller islands to the south. Sparse scraggy vegetation grows in patches along its length. It is home to a small community of scraggy ex-pats who blend in well with the environs. If it were not for one fact, the island would be lost in the backwaters of the Bahamas. The how's and why's that made Norman's Cay the most infamous island in all the Bahamas is a story that is told and retold in print, movie, and documentary. It is a story that captures the imagination. The story has everything: mystery, murder, drugs, international intrigue, sex, deception, money, money and more money.

In 1970 Carlos Lehder, the hard nosed co-founder of the Medellin drug cartel, purchased a large portion of Norman's Cay. At the time of his $4.5 million investment in Bahamian real estate there was a sparse population of foreign nationals living on the island. Carlos purchased his holding on the island with the complete blindfolded cooperation of the Bahamian government. He did not arrive on the scene to build a new Club Med. The residents of Norman's would soon discover his inspired motives. Days after his purchase he made generous offers to the residents to purchase their property. Most sold out. A few steadfast residents held onto their piece of paradise. The many that left with money in hand were the lucky majority. Within weeks of Carlos's generous offer to purchase all the deeds, the remaining holdouts began to have health problems. One couple was found in their cockpit floating at sea with their throats slit. Bodies were found washed up on an adjacent island. Within a month, all of the previous residents of Norman's Cay left with cash in their pockets and a smile on their face or were never seen alive again. Carlos swelled with pride in his recent acquisition.

The first stage of Carlos Lehder's master plan to turn Norman's Cay into the Medellin drug cartel's transshipment port for drugs smuggled into Florida went surprisingly well. A palatial mansion was constructed overlooking the bay for Carlos and his inner circle. Quarters for the security detail stretched along the beach. A beautiful new dock was built for the visiting Bahamian Coast Guard who kept the cruisers away for a small consideration. The Coast Guard hadn't had this much fun since American Prohibition. The friendly Bahamian bankers also did their best to be as accommodating as possible to the financial needs of their new foreign client. Only 300 miles from Florida it was the perfect spot to do a bit of drug running and money laundering at the height of the 'War on Drugs'.

Norman's Cay

This would just be another story of 'business man makes good on his tropical island' if it weren't for the curiosity of American intelligence: the State Department, the FBI, NSA and the international policing agency Interpol. The island just south of Norman's Cay and five hundred feet from Carlos's front door was acquired by a fun loving band of loosely affiliated international law enforcement agencies. The acquisition of this counter intelligence island observation post was facilitated by the Bahamian government. Just like in the casinos in Freeport, the house never loses. The double dipping Bahamian officials seized the day and became everyone's friend. The intelligence community built and populated their observation post almost concurrently with the construction that took place on the other side of the bay at Carlos's North American headquarters of the Medellin drug cartel.

While Carlos luxuriated in the drug-fueled opulence of the world he had created, the various intelligence agencies from the US and around the world had to be content with Quonset style housing transported in on landing craft and helicopter. The good guys had something that the bad guys didn't have. The supplies for the listening post included state-of-the-art short distance radar, airplane transponder tracking devices, and cameras with powerful zoom lens. They had everything that a dedicated intelligence group would need to spy on their next door neighbor. The spy post could track the daily arrival of drug planes with their short distance radar. They could record the plane's radio communications with Norman islanders. They could photograph the plane and identify the manufacturer, make and model of the plane minutes before the plane's wheels touched the runway. With extremely accurate intelligence the listening post communicated with the FBI database, very often identifying the owner of the plane. In short American intelligence knew more about the planes that landed than Carlos did.

In a very short period of time the island became the largest transshipment port for illegal drugs in the northern hemisphere. Planes flew in constantly. They dropped off sacks of money. Then they refueled and were back in the air within hours. On take off the plane and pilot were photographed. If the plane's transponder was turned on it was tracked. American intelligence then used their short range radar to send the plane's vector to Miami air control and Homestead Air Force base in southern Florida. They would pick up the plane and follow its vector. If the pilot flew high enough then radar could follow it straight to the landing strip.

Carlos spent millions of dollars to transport cocaine to Florida. U.S. and international intelligence spent millions to staff a listening post 500 feet from Carlos. While American politicians were clamoring for more and more dollars to fight a 'War on Drugs' the ever vigilant well-tanned intelligence community just south of Carlos remained eerily quiet. In complacent cooperation with the Bahamian government they watched but did not disturb a most lucrative criminal enterprise.

The cordial relationship between Carlos, the US and Bahamas could have been an enduring friendship if Carlos hadn't decided to get into politics, more precisely if he hadn't started assassinating politicians. Carlos Lehder founded the National Latino Movement, a Columbian political party which maintained three congressional seats. The political party's main purpose was to oppose extradition. It wasn't until April 30, 1984 with the assassination of Rodrigo Lara Bonilla, the Colombian Minister of Justice that all his friends began to bail. The President of Panama, Manuel Noriega, tried to strike a deal with the US government for amnesty by informing on Carlos. After many fruitful years of cordial business dealings, the Bahamian Government then turned on Carlos and indicted him for bribing Bahamian officials. The whole enterprise unraveled and Carlos became a ward of the US prison system. Carlos was out of the drug business. He had his sentence reduced to 55 years for testifying against Manuel Noriega who was promptly convicted in a US court. The listening post was stripped to the foundation. American Air Force attack helicopters were sent to Norman's Cay to strafe and redecorate Carlos's palatial estate with air to surface missiles.

Twenty years later Quest quietly motored through the tricky dogleg entrance to the anchorage at Norman's Cay. On our right was the bare stretch of land with the remains of the spying outpost. Directly to our left were the eerie bombed remains of Carlos's castle by the sea. Keeping eyes straight ahead we sought out a quiet stretch of anchorage in the channel between the islands. The anchorage was surprisingly empty and very narrow. All of the boats had a second anchor deployed in the traditional Bahamian anchoring style. We set our first bow anchor and then rigged the second anchor from the bow and carried it fifty feet behind the stern in the dinghy and dug it into the sandy bottom. With Quest's anchors well set Wendy stowed the sailing gear while I set to build a cheese, onion, sun-dried tomato, basil and broccoli panzone in the galley. A storm was brewing in the Atlantic. We would stay a few days at Norman's until it blew through. Just after sunset the wind began to pick up and continued to build all night. In the morning the anemometer read thirty five knots of wind but the surface of the anchorage was placid.

"Shall we go pay our respects to Carlos?" I asked Wendy.

As we motored in front of the mansion we couldn't help but notice that a fifty foot Bahamian Coast Guard patrol boat had taken shelter from the storm and was moored to the dock. We tied to the dock and climbed up on the dock's plank deck.

"Look at the bridge of the patrol boat" I said to Wendy. "The officer is asleep at the wheel."

The captain of the patrol boat, head back, feet resting on the steering wheel, cap pulled over his eyes was sound asleep in dream land. He hadn't even heard us approaching in the dinghy.

"Let's go talk to him" I said to Wendy.

"You go talk to him" she replied.

Wendy started walking for the beach and I continued to the moored patrol boat at the end of the pier. The door to the wheel house was wide open.

"Morning" I said in a loud voice.

The officer sat up in the chair. His cap fell on the deck and his hand snapped to his sidearm.

"This must be like the good old days" I said.

He reached down and recovered his cap. He then slid down in the seat, put the cap over his eyes, put his legs up on the instrument panel and resumed his repose. I quietly walked back the way I had come down the hundred foot dock.

"So what did he have to say?" Wendy asked.

"He was pretty talkative" I said. "Great guy. He invited us down to Nassau for his New Year's bash."

"Sure he did. Did you think that he was going to shoot you?" Wendy asked.

"Never, he would have missed anyway. I was standing a full five feet away" I joked.

With the exception of patrol boat 42 and its snoozing crew the island seemed deserted. We had formed a rough plan for our visit to the island that morning while eating breakfast. We would save the mansion for last. First we would stretch our legs on the landing strip. We climbed the beach. Directly to our right were the one-room shanties that Carlos had built for the workers and security staff. We skirted the bluff where the mansion sat and made for the runway. To our complete surprise when we arrived at the runway a number of roughly constructed shacks were built about fifty feet from the blacktop edge. Right in the center of the dwellings was a restaurant... a restaurant? The primitive structure was built from branches of a jacaranda tree with palm fronds for walls. There was a crudely painted 'OPEN' sign hanging askew above the makeshift entrance.

"Let's go have a soda" I said to Wendy.

The day was already starting to heat up.

"A cold drink would be great right now" she said.

We stooped to enter the restaurant doorway and adjusted our eyes to a dark windowless one room shack about twenty by twenty feet. Six small un-matching tables were scattered about the dirt floor. A young man in his mid-twenties lay sprawled over the bar sound asleep. His long dirty blond hair cascaded over his face and draped halfway down the bar. We sat and giggled for a couple of minutes. I rapped on the table.

The barkeep looked up and said in a thoroughly California accent "Where did you two come from?"

"We just flew in" I said.

"Wow man, I didn't hear a thing. You should have been here last night. We partied with the Coast Guard until two in the morning. Man did we get blasted."

"So that's why the Coast Guard is still at the dock" I said.

"Yeah they're still probably too drunk to go anywhere" he said.

"What do you have to drink?" I asked.

"We drank everything last night man" he said.

"How about a glass of water?" I said.

"Sure man."

He reached around the bar, dumped out last night's contents of two glasses and filled them with water.

"Here you go" he said. "That will be two bucks."

"A dollar for a glass of water?" I asked.

"No, four bucks. It's two bucks each" he said.

Norman's Cay

I threw a five on the table and walked out.

At the door I turned around and said "You drink the water. It might do you some good."

"Thanks man" he said.

A sketchy picture of Norman's Cay was beginning to come into focus as we walked back down the landing strip to Carlos's former Bahamian retreat. The house sat on a bluff overlooking the anchorage. There was a concrete and stone pathway pleasantly meandering directly to the front door. It wasn't until we got close that we made out the immense size of the house. We passed through the empty door frame. The shattered door was lying against the wall. The magnificent curved bay window that overlooked the anchorage was destroyed. Broken glass covered the floor. Large artillery had blown big holes in the steel-reinforced concrete walls. Other than that, it looked pretty normal. The pilots that strafed and shelled the building did a haphazard job.

The rest of the house was much intact. Wendy walked to the back of the house to look at the bedrooms. I stayed in the living room. I sat down on the edge of the indoor fire pit and closed my eyes. The history and ghosts of the past were haunting every inch of the living room. It was deathly quiet. It was New Year's Eve. With my eyes closed I could hear the clinking of glasses, the boisterous bravado of a coked up Carlos as he toasted his success and the success of his enterprise. I could imagine the pig being roasted on a spit in the fire pit, bags of cocaine strewn about the coffee tables, scantily clad women and guests so high they were bouncing off the walls.

I walked into the kitchen. Pots sat on the stove and were hanging on racks. There was even cutlery in the drawers. As I stood in the kitchen, looking over the counter into the living room, I wondered about the twenty five men from American Intelligence stationed five hundred feet away. Could someone as egotistical and mad on cocaine as Carlos was reported to be, resist taunting the government that was spying on him? Especially at Christmas, did he ever have one of his underlings dinghy over to the other side of the bay with a case of Scotch and a few cases of Columbian beer?

The more I thought about it the more I convinced myself that his relationship with the US at that time may have been relatively cordial. These were troubled times with soured relationships in the Americas. Columbia fractured from the inside from the ever increasing power of the drug lords. An American population couldn't seem to get enough of Carlos's magic white powder. Contras and the CIA were fighting a losing war in Nicaragua. There was even possible collaboration between the drug kingpins and the CIA to transport drugs in exchange for arms to the contras. President Manuel Noriega was employed by the CIA to maintain a strong democracy in Panama while the Panamanian banks laundered drug money.

These were exciting times. And this room was the epicenter for discussions of geopolitical importance on a very large scale. Putting only a few pieces of the puzzle together it would seem absurd to think that the federales that lived across the bay were not invited to Carlos's Christmas parties. They would have been highly insulted if not invited. There is Mister R. from the State department over in the corner talking to the topless bimbo. There is Mister G. in the kitchen stirring a pot of paella and talking to Carlos's mistress.

Wendy came out from the bedroom.

"This place is a real bore" she said. "Lets get out of here, it's just a bombed out wreck."

The spell was broken.

"Yes you are right. It is just a bombed out wreck" I said.

We walked down the path from the front door to the dock. Very silently we passed the patrol captain soundly sleeping in the cockpit. I wasn't as full of bravado as when we first landed beside the dock. Just being in a place where so many lives were destroyed was haunting. We pushed off the dock. When we were far enough away not to wake the party-weary Coast Guard, I started the engine and we headed back to Quest, our floating island of neutrality.

Twenty

Georgetown

On the trailing edge of the storm that carried us to Norman's Cay we pulled up anchor. With all sails full and Quest heeling at forty-five degrees we streaked through the crystal opalescent waters of the sheltered Bahama Banks to the beautiful anchorage at Warderick Wells. The Warderick Wells group of islands comprises one of the few land and sea parks in the Bahamas. Because of this status, anchoring and mooring is controlled and strictly enforced. We picked up our assigned mooring practically in front of the visitors center. To our surprise when we climbed the hill to pay our mooring fee the park personnel were all American cruisers that had came to visit, but fell in love with the natural beauty. In such a wonderful place I expected to see Bahamians.

"Are all the Bahamians on Christmas leave?" I asked the ranger.

The entire staff in the office snapped their heads in our direction.

"Come out on the porch and sit down" said the assistant ranger.

Georgetown

The porch overlooked a cut between an adjacent island. The tidal currents keep a fairly wide channel open where the moorings are installed. There was every shade of light blue. It was breathtaking. The ranger station was high on a rocky bluff and had a great view of the banks. Ranger Wayne briefly explained the situation.

"Warderick Wells is a marine park that is supported by donations from American and other international sources. The Bahamian government does not really encourage our activity nor do they hinder them. Their approach is: do good things and don't get into trouble. Bahamians are not really interested in working in the park. That is why we employ foreigners almost exclusively. I hope that you have a great stay and have a happy New Year."

Don't get into trouble? What could that mean in the Bahamas? You were too stupid to destroy the incriminating evidence?

Our stay in the Bahamas was a treat for the eyes and food for the imagination. Although the Bahamian electorate goes through the motions of electing a representative form of government, their elected officials interpret the law in a most generous fashion. One is left with the impression that the rules of governance are drafted from the pages of crime novels and pirate movies. No country in the world has perfect laws, perfect leaders and a perfect citizenry. Most countries do strive to at least polish and redefine the darker patches of their history. The Bahamas embrace a nefarious past where pirating is the prime driver of their business model. The Bahamas exist only a short distance from America but the cultural and political differences between the countries is staggering. Economically dependent on banking and tourism, they have made a splendid success from blue water, geographical isolation and the idiosyncratic pursuits of foreign nationals.

During three months of full time cruising in the Bahamas we had gone out of our way to seek out remote anchorages. Warderick Wells was intriguing and beautiful. It was also a slice of American civilization. The anchoring restrictions and daily park fees were not our style. Our stay was enjoyable but brief.

Two days later we pressed south along the sheltered waters of the Bahama banks. The island of Great Exuma and the city of Georgetown beckoned us. Georgetown in many ways would be an end and a beginning in the story of Quest.

From Warderick Wells, we island hopped on short day sails. Our first stop was Staniel Cay. Staniel is the second largest of the Exuma chain with a population to match. It was Christmas season and a very popular anchoring spot for winter cruisers. The anchorage near the city was filled with visiting boats. We anchored at Majors Cay a short distance from the city. After being the sole boat in many of our anchorages the thirty boats at Majors anchorage seemed like a crowd.

The high spirited Christmas season at Staniel Cay extends well into January with festivals and boat regattas. The entire island overflowed with good will and Christmas greetings. While the cruisers slept Wendy and I dropped the dinghy intending to explore the many natural caves around Majors Cay but our main interest was to visit Pig beach.

Georgetown

After three months of sailing, we finally ran into some real pigs.

Legend suggests that the original pigs that populated Pig Island were dropped off hundreds of years ago by passing pirates with the intention of retrieving their cargo after a raid on an island to the south. The pigs are still there. The pirates did not return for any number of pirate-themed reasons. Today the pigs run wild like a group of school children at recess. They swim on the beach and frolic in the waves. They luxuriate in the shade of the palms. Their status as marooned creatures has not dampened their zeal for living the good life in their tropical paradise. In addition to the island serving as a novel type of tourist attraction it is also a local dumping area. The pigs are most accommodating garbage eaters. The pig population is kept in check by the volume of edible trash dumped on the island and forays into the pig sanctuary by local poachers who thin the pig population for the tables of local restaurants under cover of darkness. Bon Appétit.

Leaving Majors Cay behind, the islands south of Staniel Cay were smaller and sparse. They did not enjoy the stature of Pig Island or the cosmopolitan nature of Georgetown. They were home to a few Bahamian nationals. Most of this bejeweled necklace of sparkling islands had been sold outright by the Bahamian government to foreign interests. Selling land is a very significant source of revenue for the Bahamas. In this short archipelago of 25 miles, the list of purchasers is a 'who's who' of the world's wealthiest. There are a lot of dreams packed into this group of rocky islands.

Our next stop was the anchorage at Great Guana Cay. A standout feature of this island at the time we were visiting was a three story castle that a couple from California had built as their island retreat. They had purchased their five acres several years ago and began hauling all the necessary supplies to the island by landing craft and cargo containers at tremendous cost. They had few visitors and were more than eager to show us around the castle. Designed by a California architect it looked pretty good for a one-family detached castle. Its striking appearance would not have been out of place in an English country side. The high turreted roof was covered with wind generators and solar panels which supplied power for their power hungry appliances. They had it all. Two sets of washers and dryers, electric heating and AC, dish washers, freezers, refrigerators, massive electric stoves: all the conveniences that one would expect to find in a luxury house on Malibu beach in Southern California.

The castle was near one of the many stalled land development projects in the Exumas. The developers planned to cut a channel through the isthmus of the island and put in a big marina. There were many land development projects that were started and abandoned in the central Exumas. In almost every case an over-enthusiastic sales pitch could not overcome economic reality. All of the unsuccessful projects had the same haunting nature. Dusty partially graded roads led you in circles. The entire site was absent of human life. The faded five by three foot sign that welcomed you to the 'Best of the Bahamas' stood mocking the folly of man. Another failed project was the only reminder of a plan that for any number of excuses had not come to fruition.

Despite all of the developers' financial roadblocks and failures, they refuse to believe that their projects are stone cold dead. The sites are ghost towns. Construction crews have left with no plans to return. The sites are managed by crusty weathered watchmen that generally succumb to the isolation and alcoholism.

Without dropping a beat the developers and their PR companies continue to market the projects as if it they were move-in ready. In every major city on the American east coast, you can find glossy brochures touting another Island Paradise that is ready for you to live your dream. These are the Fabulous Vaporware Islands of the Exumas. Take perfectly rational northern urban dwellers that fight a blizzard to get to the airport, then three hours later drop them into a sun filled dream and it becomes an irresistible reality.

Our favorite example of the 'Perfect Paradise Island' was Cave Cay. We anchored off the beach of Cave Cay to avoid an approaching storm. The following day we dinghied into a half completed dredged channel into a half completed marina only to be confronted by a one quarter complete project. We wandered around the skeleton of a club house and the half completed houses on the bluff. We wandered for a full hour before a sole watchman approached us.

"You ain't supposed to be here. This is private" he barked at us from about twenty feet away.

"Put up your hands Wendy. He's got us surrounded" I barked back.

His mood mellowed significantly. He probably hadn't seen another human for weeks. Everything indicated that construction had been halted months or years ago.

"What's going on here?" I asked.

He launched into the well packaged sales brochure pitch. "This island is completely sold out. Everybody important owns property here. We are in the last stage of dredging the channel to an average depth of ten feet." He pointed to the rusted remains of a dredging barge half sunk at the back corner of the half completed marina. "The air strip will be completed next week."

The airstrip was a weedy strip of crudely graded sand that was not prepared for commercial flights.

"See that house on the bluff? That is the private residence of the developer. He drops in all the time to party."

Apparently the developer, also known as 'The Wizard of Oz', was prepared to live and party in a house without doors, windows and siding. The watchman, developers and marketing firm live in a perpetual web of fantasy. It is only the construction workers that have the sense to stay away.

"Where are all of the workmen, the heavy equipment, the building materials?" I asked.

"The workers are on vacation. They'll be back next week."

We excused ourselves, got into the dinghy and returned to Quest. Five hundred feet to the south of Cave

Cay, Musha Cay was in complete economic contrast to the stalled developments in the Exumas. At the time of our visit Musha Cay was a private island with strictly enforced property rights. The entire island was owned and maintained by a very wealthy Chicago industrialist. We approached the island. A security unit met us at the beach. They were polite but unyielding. We were not going to set foot on the island. David Copperfield subsequently purchased the island in 2007 to turn it into yet another tropical paradise resort. David Copperfield has made 747's disappear and elephants vanish. Let's give him some time to work his magic. Maybe he can turn the deserted sands of Musha Cay into gold.

The entire time that we were in the Exumas we had sailed over the Exuma Banks. The Banks are on the western side of the Exuma chain. There are many reasons to sail the Banks. They have beautiful turquoise waters. All of the anchorages are on the Banks side of the islands. One reason that attracts most boaters to the Banks is its placid waters. On days that the Atlantic is raging, water on the Banks is flat calm. It was impossible for Quest to sail any further on the Banks. At six feet, Quest's draft was too deep for the shallow Banks south of Cave Cay.

Our sailing plan was to exit the cut between Cave Cay and Musha Cay and sail the Atlantic side down to Children's Bay Cay. Our estimated trip time was four hours. The cut at Children's Cay had a fine entrance at high tide but shallowed to a marginal five feet at low tide. An 8 AM departure from Cave Cay would put us at Children's Cay at high tide. We pulled up the anchor without anticipation and made for the narrow cut between Cave Cay and Musha Cay. The actual width of the channel was about forty feet.

When we were within sight of the cut our relaxed mood turned to watchfulness. The current in the cut was very swift. I pulled Quest back to build up some speed before we hit the current. I entered the stream between the cut at about six knots and a moderate engine speed. The moment Quest hit the stream Quest's forward momentum slowed then stopped. I looked down at the depth gauge. Had we run up on a sand bar? No, there were two feet of water under the keel. I eased the throttle forward. Quest refused to budge. It was a very eerie feeling to be in the cut with Cave Cay on our left and Musha Cay on our right with the engine revving and not moving an inch. I opened the throttle wide. The engine raced. Our speed didn't increase. We had no forward motion.

At that moment I thought that the battle to reach the ocean was lost for the day. I would have to retreat. Then I thought of one last trick. In a channel with a swift current, the mass of the water is in the center. The sides of a channel have a reduced current or even a counter current. I turned Quest ever so slowly to port and into the shallower waters at the side of the cut. We didn't exactly bolt forward. We inched forward. The cut was about two hundred feet long. Our speed didn't even register on the GPS. It took an entire hour to claw our way out of the cut. We sailed down to Children's Cay for a one night stay before moving on to Georgetown.

At the height of the winter cruising season Georgetown is a magnet for boaters from the American and Canadian east coasts. Expect no culture shock in Georgetown in this busy holiday season unless you are a Bahamian. The anchorages were over crowded and a buzz of activity. Dinghies crisscrossed the bay at top speed hauling water skiers behind them and turning the air blue with two cycle engine fumes. The decks of anchored boats were crowded with revelers. Every channel on the VHF was saturated with chatter about recipes for how to cook a turkey on an alcohol stove to repairing a water pump. For the crew of Quest who intentionally sought out the solace of isolation, this was an assault on our sensibility. We sailed past at least 250 anchored boats and anchored well south of this busy hive of humanity.

One could easily guess the reason for Georgetown's popularity from looking at a chart. It is the largest, most well-equipped anchorage in the Exumas. Georgetown is a vibrant small city filled with everything that a huge cruising population needs to enjoy the season. On the critical list of supplies for all cruisers are liquor, food and boat parts. Many times all three items were sold in the same store. Georgetown and the boating community is a happy place to be in the winter. There is an esprit de corps that can not be rivaled. If one is inclined to the social life they will be kept busy from the sunrise yoga classes on the beach at dawn to the all night parties in the many clubs on the various islands surrounding Great Exuma Island. A VHS cruiser radio net devotes several channels on a 24 hour basis to updates on new arrivals and the prices of Johnny Walker at the plethora of liquor stores in town. There were even classes on the radio devoted to engine maintenance. It was a hospitality saturated environment.

The winter cruisers were living busy lives in Paradise. They were so entirely occupied that I doubt a single one gave a moment's notice to our lack of social intentions. Our approach to the social life at Georgetown was not the only thing that set us apart from the community. The great majority of cruisers were at their final destination. They would fully enjoy their stay in Georgetown. They would then spend a week hugging and saying their good byes to a hundred close friends. With the threat of hurricanes looming in the summer they would sail north to Florida and put their boat on the hard for another hurricane season, take a flight north to their homes and resume the land lubber's life. They would return the following season and repeat the process.

Georgetown is the end of the road for winter cruisers for another reason. Once you leave the sheltered waters and the embrace of the Georgetown boating community and travel south, you are all alone in a big, big sea. An adventure south of Georgetown meant the ultimate peril. The Atlantic, with huge ocean swells and fierce storms, did not beckon the winter visitors of Georgetown. The revelers in Georgetown had found their place in the sun. Among these happy boaters there was no resolve to disturb a perfectly good thing and taunt the fickle forces of nature on the open North Atlantic.

Wendy and I had spent the last three months learning to sail on our first shake down cruise. Quest had performed magnificently. We fared reasonably well in the sheltered waters of the Bahamas. We had grown our confidence. In our minds we were ready for the trials of the ocean. While anchored in the calm waters of Georgetown we did not plan any final destination. It was the odyssey of the journey that attracted us. It was the allure of foreign ports that sustained our momentum. Our plans were vague. We would do whatever it took to sail below the hurricane belt which the insurance companies defined as the south coast of Grenada and just north of Trinidad. Our sailing future at that moment seemed absolutely open. It would be the highly uncertain vagaries of wind and water that would ultimately shape our plans.

We motored to Georgetown for the final time to fill the dinghy full of the supplies necessary to sustain us until we made our way to the Dominican Republic. With 200 plus cruisers in the anchorage the selection of food and libations was quite extraordinary for the Bahamas. A brisk trade kept the prices a bit low in comparison to the majority of the Exumas. Accustomed to many years of welcoming cruisers the Bahamian merchants were friendly and accommodating. We bought our supplies. We traded books at the book exchange. We wandered the city knowing that it would be the last civilization that we would see for several months. Our final stop was the Customs and Immigration house. We walked into the two hundred year old building and were greeted by a very friendly Bahamian Customs Officer. She glanced at our passports.

"You've been in the Bahamas a long time" she said.

"We've traveled from north to south" I replied.

"In my entire life I have never left Georgetown. Where are you going next?" she asked.

"Wendy and I are leaving tomorrow for the Turks and Caicos."

"Can I come with you?" she asked as she stamped our passport.

The End

The Quest Series continues with
'Quest on the Thorny Path'

www.questandcrew.com

Glossary

AGM battery (Chapter 12 – Zero G) – Absorbed Glass Mat battery. To store electrical power, boats generally carry batteries. An AGM battery is a sealed battery that is ideal for a boat because it does not require ventilation, can be mounted in any orientation, and does not require constant maintenance. Quest had an AGM 'house' battery' under each settee in the salon and two smaller starter batteries for the Yanmar engine in the cockpit lazarette.

Anemometer (Chapter 1 – Hurricane) – An anemometer measures wind speed. Quest's anemometer was manufactured by Raymarine. It sat on the top of the mast and was connected to displays in the cockpit and nav station via Raytheon cabling.

Barometer (Chapter 1 – Hurricane) – A barometer measures atmospheric pressure and so helps predict weather changes. A falling barometer means that the pressure is lowering. A sudden drop in atmospheric pressure over a few hours generally forecasts an approaching storm. Hurricanes have very low pressures. The lower the pressure, the greater the winds and more intense the storm. The normal sea level pressure in the US is 1013.25 mb. The worst hurricanes on record have a central pressure of 882- 892 mb with winds 175-200 mph. When Ivan passed over Quest, our barometer was below 900 mb

Bilge (Chapter 3 – A Two Ton Paperweight) – The bilge is the part of the boat below the removable floorboards. Most of it is below the waterline. It is the compartment formed by the two sides curving down to the keel. On Quest, the bilge under the salon was shallow and housed the waste and diesel tanks. Under the engine, the bilge was very deep and narrow and was where any uncontained liquid eventually collected, to be pumped out by the bilge pump. Bilges often smell if waste and engine oil are not properly contained, as was the case when Quest was first purchased.

Bobstay (Chapter 9 – Pirate Island) – A bobstay is a strong rope, wire, or chain connecting the end of the bowsprit (the pole or platform extending from a sailboat's bow) to a lower part of the boat's bow. The bobstay holds the bowsprit down against the counteracting force of the forestay which holds the mast up. On Quest, the bobstay was made from a very strong, thick, twisted stainless steel architectural wire called Dyform

Bowditch (Chapter 4 – After the Hurricane: Welcome to Trinidad & Chapter 8: Echo and the Big Black Whale) Bowditch is a boating manual originally written by Nathaniel Bowditch and first published in 1802. It is an encyclopedia of navigation that is the size of a Bible. It covers ever possible procedure on boating. Though its real title is the American Practical Navigator, the book today is commonly referred to as Bowditch. It can be found on most commercial and military vessels in the world.

Can – see also Nun (Chapter 8: Echo and the Big Black Whale) A can-shaped buoy marks the right side of the channel leaving a harbor. It is green with odd numbers

Glossary

Chine (Chapter 12 – Zero G) The Chine is the curved side of a boat's hull.

Dynaplate (Chapter 10 - The Splash) – A dynaplate is a bronze ground plate used to provide electric ground for single sideband receivers. A dynaplate lets the water surrounding the boat serve as "counterpoise", a substitute for earth 'ground'.

Fiddles (Chapter 14 - Florida Farewell) Fiddles are movable steel bars fitted to the top of a marine stove. They are clamped around a pot so that it remains secure in a seaway.

Gunwales – Gunwales are the top edge of the side of a boat. In old sailing ships, guns were mounted on the strong gunwales.

Halyard (Chapter 12 – Zero G) A halyard is a rope used for raising and lowering a sail. It is attached to the top of a sail and is attached to a cleat once the sail is raised. The term comes from 'to haul yards'.

Lazy Jack (Chapter 12 – Zero G) Lazy jacks are a system of light ropes used to neatly cradle the mainsail when it is lowered onto the boom to keep the sail from falling off the boom onto the deck.

Mal de Mare (Chapter 12 – Zero G) is seasickness. Seasickness is caused by repetitive angular and linear acceleration and deceleration. Being sick on a boat generally starts with nausea caused by motion. Motion sickness can have many symptoms besides nausea: primarily abdominal discomfort, vomiting, and dizziness. Symptoms are sometimes preceded by yawning, hyperventilation, salivation, pallor, cold sweating and sleepiness. Other symptoms include headache, swallowing air, fatigue, weakness and inability to concentrate.

Mast shoe (Chapter 9 – Pirate Island) The mast is seated inside the hull into a wooden block or shoe to keep it stable. Traditionally, small keepsakes are thrown into the mast shoe before mounting the mast to ensure good luck.

Millibar – see also Barometer. (Chapter 1 – Hurricane) Barometers use millibars to measure atmospheric pressure.

Norseman fittings (Chapter 9 – Pirate Island) Norseman fittings are swageless mechanical terminals attached to each end of a wire to make rigging. Unlike a swage terminal which requires a special machine to crimp it onto a wire, a swageless terminal can be attached easily. This makes them very useful if the wire assembly must be made-up on site, at sea, or by a do-it-yourselfer.

Nun – see also Can (Chapter 8: Echo and the Big Black Whale) A nun is a cone-shaped buoy that marks the left side of the channel when leaving a harbor. It is red with even numbers. When entering a harbor, the common expression 'red right returning' helps the sailor remember how to navigate.

On the hard (Chapter 2 – A funny thing happened on the way to buy a boat & Chapter 10 – The Splash) When a sailboat is hauled out of water and blocked on stands, it rests 'on the hard' surface instead of on the water.

Packing Gland (Chapter 3 – A Two Ton Paperweight & Chapter 10 – The Splash) - The propeller shaft exits the stern of the vessel. The shaft is naturally under water. A boat needs a way to keep the shaft spinning and at the same time keep the water out of the boat. The packing gland firmly fits around the shaft and provides a water tight seal.

Pirogue (Chapter 5 – Chacachacare) – A pirogue is a traditional shallow draft Trinidadian boat designed for fishing. It is made from wood and fitted with a modern outboard engine.

Pulpit (Chapter 11 – Hello North Palm Beach) – The pulpit is the metal framework at the bow of a boat which extends past the deck. It serves as an attachment for the lifelines and provides a safety railing when standing on the anchor platform over the bowsprit.

Re-rig (Chapter 9 – Pirate Island) A boat has wires that hold up the mast. This is the standing rigging. When the wire gets tired and stressed over time, it must be replaced. Re-rigging is replacing the standing rigging. It is a very big complicated enterprise.

Rhumb line (Chapter 8: Echo and the Big Black Whale) A rhumb is a path that will take you from one point on the earth to another if you maintain a constant bearing. A rhumb line is a steady course or line of bearing that appears as a straight line on a chart.

Sheet Block (Chapter 5 – Chacachacare: The Leper Colony) A block on a boat is another word for a pulley. If it is a sheet block then the sheet line runs through the block. A sheet line is in general terms a line that controls the trim of a sail. Therefore, the main sheet block is the block/pulley that controls the main sheet line. The main sheet is the sail that is in the center of a sloop.

Shroud (Chapter 9 – Pirate Island) – Shrouds are wires that hold a mast up from side to side. A shroud is part of a sailboat's rigging.

Stay (Chapter 9 – Pirate Island) – Stays are wires that hold a spar (like the mast or bowsprit) tight. For a mast, they are in front of the mast (forestay) and behind the mast (backstay), running from the top of the mast to the hull. Stays are part of a boat's rigging.

Survey (Chapter 2 – A funny thing happened on the way to buy a boat) – A marine survey is a detailed inspection of all parts of a boat to determine its overall condition. They are very useful when buying a boat. Insurance companies require periodic surveys.

Swages, Swageless terminal (Chapter 9 – Pirate Island) See also Norseman Fittings. A swage is a tool for bending cold metal to a required shape. A swageless terminal does not require a swage to crimp the terminal onto wire. Norseman fittings are examples of swageless terminals used in rigging.

Tack – (Chapter 8: Echo and the Big Black Whale) In sailing, a tack is how a boat is aligned to the wind when the bow is pointed into the wind. If the wind is from starboard, then the boat is on a "starboard tack", and if from port, on "port tack". When we 'make our tack', we swing the wheel and let the wind shift the sails to the other side of the boat and so move onto another angle of wind, e.g. from a starboard tack to a port tack.

Tuning (the rig) (Chapter 9 – Pirate Island) Tuning a rig involves placing the mast in the right position in the boat with the proper amount of tension applied to the shrouds and stays. It can be a very complex process, especially in racing sailboats, involving loosening and tightening turnbuckles to get the proper bend on the mast and tension on all wires.

Windlass (Chapter 10- The Splash) A Windlass is a type of winch used on boats to hoist anchors. We replaced Quest's windlass with a 1000 watt Lofrans windlass which could handle rope or chain anchor lines.

Yankee (Chapter 12 – Zero G) A yankee is the smaller of the two sails at the bow on a cutter rig, specifically the fore-sail flying above and forward of the larger jib sail.

49108320R00153

Made in the USA
San Bernardino, CA
20 August 2019